Irish Fireside
Tales

Thank you, Dee,
for your generosity
and your kindness

Fynn McCool

Helen.

IRISH FIRESIDE TALES

MYTHS · LEGENDS · FOLKTALES

Edited by LESLIE CONRON

Madison Park Press
New York

Developed by Arena Books Associates, LLC

This edition first published by Madison Park Press
by arrangement with Arena Books Associates, LLC.

Photographs from The Irish Image Collection.

ISBN: 978-1-58288-262-8

Sources:
Lady Gregory. *Gods and Fighting Men,* 1904.
Lady Gregory. *Cuchulain of Muirthemne*, 1902.
Lady Wilde. *Ancient Legends, Mystic Charms, & Superstitions of Ireland*, 1887.
William Carleton. *Traits & Stories of the Irish Peasantry,* 1896.
Thomas Crofton Croker. *Fairy Legends and Traditions of the South of Ireland*, 1825.
Patrick Kennedy. *The Fireside Stories of Ireland*, 1870.
Jeremiah Curtin. *Myths and Folk-Lore of Ireland*, 1890.

The following tales—"The Fate of the Children of Lir," "The Coming of Finn,"
"Finn's House," "Diarmuid and Grania: The Flight from Teamhair," "Diarmuid and
Grania: The Pursuit"— are from *Gods and Fighting Men* by Lady Gregory.

The Cuchulain tales—"The Dream of Angus Og," "The Birth of Cuchulain," "Boy
Deeds of Cuchulain," "The Courting of Emer," "The War for the Bull of
Cuailgne"—are from *Cuchulain of Muirthemne* by Lady Gregory.

The rest of the tales are from the appropriate sources listed above.

Contents

Introduction

It's a given: The Irish are story-tellers. They know well how to talk, and they know just as well how to listen. And they surely know a good story when they hear it. There are some who say the Irish are so imaginative they can't tell a story straight: they have to invent, create, digress, fill in details—sweeten the senses, so to speak—to help you experience the story, to hear its music.

Tales told round a fire—whether ancient tales of the gods, kings, and heroes round an open campfire with a gathering of warriors or elders, or tales of the simple country folk told round a rural kitchen fireplace with a gathering of neighbors on a winter's eve—are vibrant expressions of cultural traditions and lore. The characters may be recognizable as gods and heroes or as fairies (evolved from the ancient Tuatha de Danann people, the early gods); enchantments or "spells" may figure in the action; and the environment may be Tir na n'Og (a land of perpetual youth beneath the water) or the harsh present. However they are presented, there is something of the Irish myth and legend in every Irish story.

There is no single source for the stories, old or new. They emerged from a kind of stew of incidents in the collective memories of bardic poets and wandering storytellers. The incidents of the old stories survived, though they were diffused and combined into a new form with local embellishments. Wandering bards collected stories from one locale, memorized the incidents—the skeleton of the story—and then adjusted the story in the retelling to each audience.

According to Douglas Hyde (a champion Irish folklorist, and the first president of Ireland), "professional storytellers had a trained ear, an enormous vocabulary, and complete command of the language." The heroic stories resolved into primitive folktales in the process of passing from the poet-bards to the peasant reciters of tales. Storytellers captured the voice of the people, and told the stories for their specific audiences. A tale in Kerry differs from the same tale-idea told in Wexford or Donegal.

Through the tales we are taken on an epic journey into the pagan, mythic past. Our journey, though, is guided by the early Christian scribes who recorded these tales in their manuscripts after centuries of an oral tradition. And the monks, of course, could not resist adding their own touches—ancient gods often became saints. These first written accounts were not organized; there is no one book we can turn to to find the sagas. Fragments of the text can be found in the *Book of the Dun Cow* compiled at the monastery of Clonmacnoise and *Book of Leinster*—both in the twelfth century—and in the *Yellow Book of Lecan* compiled in the late fourteenth century.

The heroic tales have been classified into four cycles or categories: the Mythological Cycle, mainly about the gods and goddesses, the divine Tuatha de Danann; the Ulster Cycle about the Knights of the Red Branch, the warriors of Ulster; the Fenian Cycle about Finn McCool and his special warrior-poets (the Fianna); and the King's Cycle about the early Irish kings. The *Tain Bo Cuailnge* (*The Cattle Raid of Cooley*) is the best known and oldest of the Ulster Cycle. It is to the Irish what *The Iliad* is to the Greeks. Cattle were a chief form of wealth to the Celts. According to the Irish legend, Queen Maeve's armies invaded Ulster to capture and bring home to Connacht the magnificent brown bull of Cooley to satisfy the Queen's need to have more possessions than her husband. And it is in this tale that we see the god-like skills of the warrior Cuchulain, the Irish Achilles.

"Ireland is a land of mists and mythic shadows," says

Lady Gregory, "of weird silences in the lonely hills, and fitful skies of deepest gloom alternating with gorgeous sunset splendors." Such an atmosphere stirs the imagination. The folktales that we read today have been imaginatively nourished and enriched by the ancient legends. And we are the better for it.

These wondrous tales are meant to be read aloud, or told to a listener. It is in the human voice that nuances and lyrical cadences are expressed. Listen as you read the story aloud and let the language sweep you along. Although storytellers no longer wander the country roads looking for an audience and a welcoming hearth, you can get a feeling of the Irish storytelling tradition by reading one of the stories yourself and then telling it to someone.

Folklorists in the late nineteenth century transcribed these tales from storytellers, some translating directly from Irish. We have retained the spelling and punctuation (though sometimes idiosyncratic and inconsistent) from each of the sources listed on the copyright page of this book. You might want to look at the glossary at the back of the book before reading the tales to acquaint yourself with some of the Irish names and places. Because the sources for these tales are many there are variations in the spelling of names and places. And there are differences in style, and use of language. Enjoy the differences. They add up to a beguiling whole.

The Fate of the Children of Lir
Lady Gregory

Now at the time when the Tuatha de Danaan chose a king for themselves after the battle of Tailltin, and Lir heard the kingship was given to Bodb Dearg, it did not please him, and he left the gathering without leave and with no word to any one; for he thought it was he himself had a right to be made king. But if he went away himself, Bodb was given the kingship none the less, for not one of the five begrudged it to him but only Lir. And it is what they determined, to follow after Lir, and to burn down his house, and to attack himself with spear and sword, on account of his not giving obedience to the king they had chosen. "We will not do that," said Bodb Dearg, "for that man would defend any place he is in; and besides that," he said, "I am none the less king over the Tuatha de Danaan, although he does not submit to me."

All went on like that for a good while, but at last a great misfortune came on Lir, for his wife died from him after a sickness of three nights. And that came very hard on Lir, and there was great talk of the death of that woman in her own time.

And the news of it was told all through Ireland, and it came to the house of Bodb, and the best of the Men of Dea were with him at that time. And Bodb said: "If Lir had a mind for it," he said, "my help and my friendship would be good for him now, since his wife is not living to him. For I have here with me the three young girls of the best shape, and the best appearance, and the best name in all Ireland, Aobh, Aoife, and Ailbhe, the three daughters of Oilell of Aran, my own three nurselings." The Men of Dea said then it was a good thought he had, and that what he said was true.

Messages and messengers were sent then from Bodb Dearg to the place Lir was, to say that if he had a mind to join with the Son of the Dagda and to acknowledge his lordship, he would give him a foster-child of his foster-children. And Lir thought well of the offer, and he set out on the morrow with fifty chariots from Sidhe Fionnachaidh; and he went by every short way till he came to Bodb's dwelling-place at Loch Dearg, and there was a welcome before him there, and all the people were merry and pleasant before him, and he and his people got good attendance that night.

And the three daughters of Oilell of Aran were sitting on the one seat with Bodb Dearg's wife, the queen of the Tuatha de Danaan, that was their foster-mother. And Bodb said: "You may have your choice of the three young girls, Lir." "I cannot say," said Lir, "which one of them is my choice, but whichever of them is the eldest, she is the noblest, and it is best for me to take her." "If that is so," said Bodb, "it is Aobh is the eldest, and she will be given to you, if it is your wish." "It is my wish," he said. And he took Aobh for his wife that night, and he stopped there for a fortnight, and then he brought her away to his own house, till he would make a great wedding-feast.

And in the course of time Aobh brought forth two children, a daughter and a son, Fionnuala and Aodh their names were. And after a while she was brought to bed again, and this time she gave birth to two sons, and they called them Fiachra and Conn. And she herself died at their birth. And that weighed very heavy on Lir, and only for the way his mind was set on his four children he would have gone near to die of grief.

The news came to Bodb Dearg's place, and all the people gave out three loud, high cries, keening their nursling. And after they had keened her it is what Bodb Dearg said: "It is a fret to us our daughter to have died, for her own sake and for the sake of the good man we gave her to, for we are thankful for his friendship and his faithfulness. However," he said, "our friendship will not be broken, for I will give him for a wife her sister Aoife."

When Lir heard that, he came for the girl and married her, and brought her home to his house. And there was honour and affection with Aoife for her sister's children; and indeed no person at all could see those four children without giving them the heart's love.

And Bob Dearg used often to be going to Lir's house for the sake of those children; and he used to bring them to his own place for a good length of time, and then he would let them go back to their own place again. And the Men of Dea were at that time using the Feast of Age in every hill of the Sidhe in turn; and when they came to Lir's hill those four children were their joy and delight, for the beauty of their appearance; and it is where they used to sleep, in beds in sight of their father Lir. And he used to rise up at the break of every morning, and to lie down among his children.

But it is what came of all this, that a fire of jealousy was kindled in Aoife, and she got to have a dislike and a hatred of her sister's children.

Then she let on to have a sickness, that lasted through nearly the length of a year. And the end of that time she did a deed of jealousy and cruel treachery against the children of Lir.

And one day she got her chariot yoked, and she took the four children in it, and they went forward towards the house of Bodb Dearg; but Fionnuala had no mind to go with her, for she knew by her she had some plan for their death or their destruction, and she had seen in a dream that there was treachery against them in Aoife's mind. But all the same she was not able to escape from what was before her.

And when they were on their way Aoife said to her people: "Let you kill now," she said, "the four children of Lir, for whose sake their father has given up my love, and I will give you your own choice of a reward out of all the good things of the world." "We will not do that indeed," said they; "and it is a bad deed you have thought of, and harm will come to you out of it."

And when they would not do as she bade them, she took out a sword herself to put an end to the children with; but she being a woman and with no good courage, and with no great strength in her mind, she was not able to do it.

They went on then west to Loch Dairbhreach, the Lake of the Oaks, and the horses were stopped there. And Aoife bade the children of Lir to go out and bathe in the lake, and they did as she bade them. And as soon as Aoife saw them out in the lake she struck them with a Druid rod, and put on them the shape of four swans, white and beautiful. And it is what she said: "Out with you, children of the king, your luck is taken away from you for ever; it is sorrowful the story will be to your friends; it is with flocks of birds your cries will be heard for ever."

And Fionnuala said: "Witch, we know now what your name is, you have struck us down with no hope of relief; but although you put us from wave to wave, there are times when we will touch the land. We shall get help when we are seen; help, and all that is best for us; even though we have to sleep upon the lake, it is our minds will be going abroad early."

And then the four children of Lir turned towards Aoife, and it is what Fionnuala said: "It is a bad deed you have done, Aoife, and it is a bad fulfilling of friendship, you to destroy us without cause; and vengeance for it will come upon you, and you will fall in satisfaction for it, for your power for our destruction is not greater than the power of our friends to avenge it on you; and put some bounds now," she said, "to the time this enchantment is to stop on us." "I will do that," said Aoife, "and it is worse for you, you to have asked it of me. And the bounds I set to your time are this, till the Woman from the South and the Man from the North will come together. And since you ask to hear it of me," she said, "no friends and no power that you have will be able to bring you out of these shapes you are in through the length of your lives, until you have been three hundred years on Loch Dairbhreach and three hundred years on Sruth na Maoile between Ireland and Alban, and three hundred years at Irrus Domnann and Inis Gluaire; and these are to be your journeys from this out," she said.

But then repentance came on Aoife, and she said: "Since there is no other help for me to give you now, you may keep your own speech; and you will be singing sweet music of the Sidhe, that would put the men of the earth to sleep, and there will be no music in the world equal to it; and your own sense and your own nobility will stay with you, the way it will not weigh so heavy on you to be in the shape of birds. And go away out of my sight now, children of Lir," she said, "with your white faces, with your stammering Irish. It is a great curse on tender lads, they to be driven out on the rough wind. Nine hundred years to be on the water, it is a long time for

any one to be in pain; it is I put this on you through treachery, it is best for you to do as I tell you now.

"Lir, that got victory with so many a good cast, his heart is a kernel of death in him now; the groaning of the great hero is a sickness to me, though it is I that have well earned his anger."

And then the horses were caught for Aoife, and the chariot yoked for her, and she went on to the palace of Bodb Dearg, and there was a welcome before her from the chief people of the place. And the son of the Dagda asked her why she did not bring the children of Lir with her. "I will tell you that," she said. "It is because Lir has no liking for you, and he will not trust you with his children, for fear you might keep them from him altogether."

"I wonder at that," said Bodb Dearg, "for those children are dearer to me than my own children." And he thought in his own mind it was deceit the woman was doing on him, and it is what he did, he sent messengers to the north to Sidhe Fionnachaidh. And Lir asked them what did they come for. "On the head of your children," said they. "Are they not gone to you along with Aoife?" he said. "They are not," said they; "and Aoife said it was yourself would not let them come."

It is downhearted and sorrowful Lir was at that news, for he understood well it was Aoife had destroyed or made an end of his children. And early in the morning of the morrow his horses were caught, and he set out on the road to the south-west. And when he was as far as the shore of Loch Dairbhreach, the four children saw the horses coming towards them, and it is what Fionnuala said: "A welcome to the troop of horses I see coming near to the lake; the people they are bringing are strong, there is sadness on them; it is us they are following, it is for us they are looking; let us move over to the shore, Aodh, Fiachra, and comely Conn. Those that are coming can be no others in the world but only Lir and his household."

Then Lir came to the edge of the lake, and he took notice of the swans having the voice of living people, and he asked them why was it they had that voice.

"I will tell you that, Lir," said Fionnuala. "We are your own four children, that are after being destroyed by your wife, and by the sister of our own mother, through the dint of her jealousy." "Is there any way to put you into your own shapes again?" said Lir. "There is no way," said Fionnuala, "for all the men of the world could not help us till we have gone through our time, and that will not be," she said, "till the end of nine hundred years."

When Lir and his people heard that, they gave out three great heavy shouts of grief and sorrow and crying.

"Is there a mind with you," said Lir, "to come to us on the land, since you have your own sense and your memory yet?" "We have not the power," said Fionnuala, "to live with any person at all from this time; but we have our own language, the Irish, and we have the power to sing sweet music, and it is enough to satisfy the whole race of men to be listening to that music. And let you stop here to-night," she said, "and we will be making music for you."

So Lir and his people stopped there listening to the music of the swans, and they slept there quietly that night. And Lir rose up early on the morning of the morrow and he made this complaint:—

"It is time to go out from this place. I do not sleep though I am in my lying down. To be parted from my dear children, it is that is tormenting my heart.

"It is a bad net I put over you, bringing Aoife, daughter of Oilell of Aran, to the house. I would never have followed that advice if I had known what it would bring upon me.

"O Fionnuala, and comely Conn, O Aodh, O Fiachra of the beautiful arms; it is not ready I am to go away from you, from the border of the harbour where you are."

Then Lir went on to the palace of Bodb Dearg, and there was a welcome before him there; and he got a reproach from Bodb Dearg for not bringing his children along with him. "My grief!" said Lir. "It is not I that would not bring my children along with me; it was Aoife there beyond, your own foster-child and the sister of their mother, that put them in the shape of four white swans on Loch Dairbhreach, in the sight of the whole of the men of Ireland; but they have their sense with them yet, and their reason, and their voice, and their Irish."

Bodb Dearg gave a great start when he heard that, and he knew what Lir said was true, and he gave a very sharp reproach to Aoife, and he said: "This treachery will be worse for yourself in the end, Aoife, than to the children of Lir. And what shape would you yourself think worst of being in?" he said.

"I would think worst of being a witch of the air," she said. "It is into that shape I will put you now," said Bodb. And with that he struck her with a Druid wand, and she was turned into a witch of the air there and then, and she went away on the wind in that shape, and she is in it yet, and will be in it to the end of life and time.

As to Bodb Dearg and the Tuatha de Danaan they came to the shore of Loch Dairbhreach, and they made their camp there to be listening to the music of the swans.

And the Sons of Gael used to be coming no less than the Men of Dea to hear them from every part of Ireland, for there never was any music or any delight heard in Ireland to compare with that music of the swans. And they used to be telling stories, and to be talking with the men of Ireland every day, and with their teachers and their fellow-pupils and their friends. And every night they used to sing very sweet music of the Sidhe; and every one that heard that music would sleep sound and quiet whatever trouble or long sickness might be on him; for every one that heard the music of the birds, it is happy and contented he would be after it.

These two gatherings now of the Tuatha de Danaan and of the Sons of Gael stopped there around Loch Dairbhreach through the length of three hundred years. And it is then Fionnuala said to her brothers: "Do you know," she said, "we have spent all we have to spend of our time here, but this one night only."

And there was great sorrow on the sons of Lir when they heard that, for they thought it the same as to be living people again, to be talking with their friends and their companions on Loch Dairbhreach, in comparison with going on the cold, fretful sea of the Maoil in the north.

And they came early on the morrow to speak with their father and with their foster-father, and they bade them farewell, and Fionnuala made this complaint:—

"Farewell to you, Bodb Dearg, the man with whom all knowledge is in pledge. And farewell to our father along with you, Lir of the Hill of the White Field.

"The time is come, as I think, for us to part from you, O pleasant company; my grief it is not on a visit we are going to you.

"From this day out, O friends of our heart, our comrades, it is on the tormented course of the Maoil we will be, without the voice of any person near us.

"Three hundred years there, and three hundred years in the bay of the men of Domnann, it is a pity for the four comely children of Lir, the salt waves of the sea to be their covering by night.

"O three brothers, with the ruddy faces gone from you, let them all leave the lake now, the great troop that loved us, it is sorrowful our parting is."

After that complaint they took to flight, lightly, airily, till they came to Sruth na Maoile between Ireland and Alban. And that was a grief to the men of Ireland, and they gave out an order that no swan was to be killed from that out, whatever chance there might be of killing one, all through Ireland.

It was a bad dwelling-place for the children of Lir they to be on Sruth na Maoile. When they saw the wide coast about them, they were filled with cold and with sorrow, and they thought nothing of all they had gone through before, in comparison to what they were going through on that sea.

Now one night while they were there a great storm came on them, and it is what Fionnuala said: "My dear brothers," she said, "it is a pity for us not to be making ready for this night, for it is certain the storm will separate us from one another. And let us," she said, "settle on some place where we can meet afterwards, if we are driven from one another in the night."

"Let us settle," said the others, "to meet one another at Carraig na Ron, the Rock of the Seals, for we all have knowledge of it."

And when midnight came, the wind came on them with it, and the noise of the waves increased, and the lightening was flashing, and a rough storm came sweeping down, the way the children of Lir were scattered over the great sea, and the wideness of it set them astray, so that no one of them could know what way the others went. But after that storm a great quiet came on the sea, and Fionnuala was alone on Sruth na Maoile; and when she took notice that her brothers were wanting she was lamenting after them greatly, and she made this complaint:—

"It is a pity for me to be alive in the state I am; it is frozen to

my sides my wings are; it is little that the wind has not broken my heart in my body, with the loss of Aodh.

"To be three hundred years on Loch Dairbhreach without going into my own shape, it is worse to me the time I am on Sruth na Maoile.

"The three I loved, Och! the three I loved, that slept under the shelter of my feathers; till the dead come back to the living I will see them no more forever.

"It is a pity I to stay after Fiachra, and after Aodh, and after comely Conn, and with no account of them; my grief I to be here to face every hardship this night."

She stopped all night there upon the Rock of the Seals until the rising of the sun, looking out over the sea on every side till at last she saw Conn coming to her, his feathers wet through and his head hanging, and her heart gave him a great welcome; and then Fiachra came wet and perished and worn out, and he could not say a word they could understand with the dint of the cold and the hardship he had gone through. And Fionnuala put him under her wings, and she said: "We would be well off now if Aodh would but come to us."

It was not long after that, they saw Aodh coming, his head dry and his feathers beautiful, and Fionnuala gave him a great welcome, and she put him under the feathers of her breast, and Fiachra under her right wing and Conn under her left wing, the way she could put her feathers over them all. "And Och! my brothers,"

she said, "this was a bad night to us, and it is many of its like are before us from this out."

They stayed there a long time after that, suffering cold and misery on the Maoil, till at last a night came on them they had never known the likes of before, for frost and snow and wind and cold. And they were crying and lamenting the hardship of their life, and the cold of the night and the greatness of the snow and the hardness of the wind. And after they had suffered cold to the end of a year, a worse night again came on them, in the middle of winter. And they were on Carraig na Ron, and the water froze about them, and as they rested on the rock, their feet and their wings and their feathers froze to the rock, the way they were not able to move from it. And they made such a hard struggle to get away, that they left the skin of their feet and their feathers and the tops of their wings on the rock after them.

"My grief, children of Lir," said Fionnuala, "it is bad our state is now, for we cannot bear the salt water to touch us, and there are bonds on us not to leave it; and if the salt water goes into our sores," she said "we will get our death." And she made this complaint:—

"It is keening we are tonight; without feathers to cover our bodies; it is cold the rough, uneven rocks are under our bare feet.

"It is bad our stepmother was to us the time she played enchantments on us, sending us out like swans upon the sea.

"Our washing place is on the ridge of the bay, in the foam

of flying manes of the sea; our share of the ale feast is the salt water of the blue tide.

"One daughter and three sons; it is in the clefts of the rocks we are; it is hard on the rocks we are, it is a pity the way we are."

However, they came on to the course of the Maoil again, and the salt water was sharp and rough and bitter to them, but if it was itself, they were not able to avoid it or to get shelter from it. And they were there by the shore under that hardship till such time as their feathers grew again, and their wings, and till their sores were entirely healed. And then they used to go every day to the shore of Ireland or of Alban, but they had to come back to Sruth na Maoile every night.

Now they came one day to the mouth of the Banna, to the north of Ireland, and they saw a troop of riders, beautiful, of the one colour, with well-trained pure white horses under them, and they travelling the road straight from the south-west.

"Do you know who those riders are, sons of Lir?" said Fionnuala.

"We do not," they said; "but it is likely they might be some troop of the Sons of Gael, or of the Tuatha de Danaan."

They moved over closer to the shore then, that they might know who they were, and when the riders saw them they came to meet them until they were able to hold talk together.

And the chief men among them were two sons of Bodb Dearg, Aodh Aithfhiosach, of the quick wits, and Fergus

Fithchiollach, of the chess, and a third part of the Riders of the Sidhe along with them, and it was for the swans they had been looking for a long while before that, and when they came together they wished one another a kind and loving welcome.

And the children of Lir asked for news of all the Men of Dea, and above all of Lir, and Bodb Dearg and their people.

"They are all well, and they are in the one place together," said they, "in your father's house at Sidhe Fionnachaidh, using the Feast of Age pleasantly and happily, and with no uneasiness on them, only for being without yourselves, and without knowledge of what happened to you from the day you left Loch Dairbhreach."

"That has not been the way with us," said Fionnuala, "for we have gone through great hardship and uneasiness and misery on the tides of the sea until this day."

And she made this complaint:—

"There is delight to-night with the household of Lir! Plenty of ale with them and of wine, although it is in a cold dwelling-place this night are the four children of the king.

"It is without a spot our bedclothes are, our bodies covered over with curved feathers; but it is often we were dressed in purple, and we drinking pleasant mead.

"It is what our food is and our drink, the white sand and the bitter water of the sea; it is often we drank mead of hazel-nuts from round four-lipped drinking cups.

"It is what our beds are, bare rocks out of the power of the waves; it is often there used to be spread out for us beds of the breast-feathers of birds.

"Though it is our work now to be swimming through the frost and through the noise of the waves, it is often a company of the sons of kings were riding after us to the Hill of Bodb.

"It is what wasted my strength, to be going and coming over the current of the Maoil the way I never was used to, and never to be in the sunshine on the soft grass.

"Fiachra's bed and Conn's bed is to come under the cover of my wings on the sea. Aodh has his place under the feathers of my breast, the four of us side by side.

"The teaching of Manannan without deceit, the talk of Bodb Dearg on the pleasant ridge; the voice of Angus, his sweet kisses; it is by their side I used to be without grief."

After that the riders went on to Lir's house, and they told the chief men of the Tuatha de Danaan all the birds had gone through, and the state they were in. "We have no power over them," the chief men said, "but we are glad they are living yet, for they will get help in the end of time."

As to the children of Lir, they went back towards their old place in the Maoil, and they stopped there till the time they had to spend in it was spent. And then Fionnuala said: "The time is come for us to leave this place. And it is to Irrus Domnann we must go now," she said, "after our three hundred years here. And indeed there will be no rest for us there, or any standing round, or any shelter from the storms. But since it is time for us to go, let us set out on the cold wind, the way we will not go astray."

So they set out in that way, and left Sruth na Maoile behind them, and went to the point of Irrus Domnann, and there they stopped, and it is a life of misery and a cold life they led there. And one time the sea froze about them that they could not move at all, and the brothers were lamenting, and Fionnuala was comforting them, for she knew there would help come to them in the end.

And they stayed at Irrus Domnann till the time they had to spend there was spent. And then Fionnuala said: "The time is come for us to go back to Sidhe Fionnachaidh, where our father is with his household and with all our own people."

"It pleases us well to hear that," they said.

O they set out flying through the air lightly till they came to Sidhe Fionnachaidh; and it is how they found the place, empty before them, and nothing in it but green hillocks and thickets of nettles, without a house, without a fire, without a hearthstone. And the four pressed close to one another then, and they gave out three sorrowful cries, and Fionnuala made this complaint:—

"It is a wonder to me this place is, and it without a house, without a dwelling-place. To see it the way it is now, Ochone! it is bitterness to my heart.

"Without dogs, without hounds for hunting, without women, without great kings; we never knew it to be like this when our father was in it.

"Without horns, without cups, without drinking in the lighted house; without young men, without riders; the way

it is to-night is a foretelling of sorrow.

"The people of the place to be as they are now, Ochone! it is grief to my heart! It is plain to my mind to-night the lord of the house is not living.

"Och, house where we used to see music and playing and the gathering of people! I think it a great change to see it lonely the way it is to-night.

"The greatness of the hardships we have gone through going from one wave to another of the sea, we never heard of the like of them coming on any other person.

"It is seldom this place had its part with grass and bushes; the man is not living that would know us, it would be a wonder to him to see us here."

However, the children of Lir stopped that night in their father's place and their grandfather's where they had been reared, and they were singing very sweet music of the Sidhe. And they rose up early on the morning of the morrow and went to Inis Gluaire, and all the birds of the country gathered near them on Loch na-n Ean, the lake of the Birds. And they used to go out to feed every day to the far parts of the country, to Inis Geadh and to Accuill, the place of Donn, son of Miled, and his people that were drowned were buried, and to all the western islands of Connacht, and they used to go back to Inis Gluaire every night.

It was about that time it happened them to meet with a young man of good race, and his name was Aibric; and he often took notice of the birds, and their singing was sweet to him and he loved them greatly, and they loved him. And it is this young man that told the whole story of all that had happened them, and put it in order.

And the story he told of what happened them in the end is this.

It was after the faith of Christ and blessed Patrick came into Ireland, that Saint Mochaomhog came to Inis Gluaire. And the first night he came to the island, the children of Lir heard the voice of his bell, ringing near them. And the brothers started up with fright when they heard it. "We do not know," they said, "what is that weak, unpleasing voice we hear."

"That is the voice of the bell at Mochaomhog," said Fionnuala; "and it is through that bell," she said, "you will be set free from pain and from misery."

They listened to that music of the bell till the matins were done, and then they began to sing the low, sweet music of the Sidhe.

And Mochaomhog was listening to them, and he prayed to God to show him who was singing that music, and it was showed to him that the children of Lir were singing it. And on the morning of the morrow he went forward to the Lake of the Birds, and he saw the swans before him on the lake, and he went down to them at the brink of the shore. "Are you the children of Lir?" he said.

"We are indeed," said they.

"I give thanks to God for that," said he, "for it is for your sakes I am come to this island beyond any other island, and let you

come to land now," he said, "and give your trust to me, that you may do good deeds and part from your sins."

They came to the land after that, and they put trust in Mochaomhog, and he brought them to his own dwelling-place, and they used to be hearing Mass with him. And he got a good smith and bade him make chains of bright silver for them, and he put a chain between Aodh and Fionnuala, and a chain between Conn and Fiachra. And the four of them were raising his heart and gladdening his mind, and no danger and no distress that was on the swans before put any trouble on them now.

Now the king of Connacht at that time was Lairgnen, son of Colman, son of Cobthach, and Deoch, daughter of Finghin, was his wife. And that was the coming together of the Man from the North and the Woman from the South, that Aoife had spoken of.

And the woman heard him talk of the birds, and a great desire came on her to get them, and she bade Lairgnen to bring them to her, and he said he would ask them of Mochaomhog. And she gave her word she would not stop another night with him unless he would bring them to her. And she set out from the house there and then. And Lairgnen sent messengers after her to bring her back, and they did not overtake her till she was at Cill Dun. She went back home with them then, and Lairgnen sent messengers to ask the birds of Mochaomhog, and he did not get them.

There was great anger on Lairgnen then, and he went himself to the place Mochaomhog was, and he asked was it true he had refused him the birds. "It is true indeed," said he. At that Lairgnen rose up, and he took hold of the swans, and pulled them off the altar, two birds in each hand, to bring them away to Deoch. But no sooner had he laid his hand on them than their bird skins fell off, and what was in their place was three lean, withered old men and a thin withered old woman, without blood or flesh.

And Lairgnen gave a great start at that, and he went out from the place. It is then Fionnuala said to Mochaomhog: "Come and baptize us now, for it is short till our death comes; and it is certain you do not think worse of parting with us than we do of parting with you. And make our grave afterwards," she said, "and lay Conn at my right side and Fiachra on my left side, and Aodh before my face, between my two arms. And pray to the God of Heaven," she said, "that you may be able to baptize us."

The children of Lir were baptized then, and they died and were buried as Fionnuala had desired; Fiachra and Conn one at each side of her, and Aodh before her face. And a stone was put over them, and their names were written in Ogham, and they were keened there, and heaven was gained for their souls.

And that is the fate of the children of Lir so far.

The Dream of Angus Og
Lady Gregory

Angus, son of the Dagda, was asleep in his bed one night, and he saw what he thought was a young girl standing near him at the top of the bed, and she the most beautiful he had ever seen in Ireland. He put out his hand to take her hand, but she vanished on the moment, and in the morning when he awoke there were no trace or tidings of her.

He got no rest that day thinking of her, and that she had gone away before he could speak to her. And the next night he saw her again, and this time she brought a little harp in her hand, the sweetest he ever heard, and she played a song to him, so that he fell asleep and slept till morning. And the same thing happened every night for a year. She would come to his bedside and be playing on the harp to him, but she would be gone before he could speak with her. And at the end

of the year she came no more, and Angus began to pine away
with love of her and with fretting after her; and he would take
no food, but lay upon the bed, and no one knew what it was ailed
him. And all the physicians of Ireland came together, but they
could not put a name on his sickness or find any cure for him.

But at last Fergne, the physician of Conn, was brought
to him, and as soon as he looked at him he knew it was not on
his body the sickness was, but on his mind. And he sent every
one away out of the room, and he said: "I think it is for the love
of some woman that you are wasting away like this." "That is
true, indeed," said Angus; "and it is my sickness has betrayed
me." And then he told him how the woman with the most
beautiful appearance of any woman in Ireland, used to come
and to be playing the harp to him through the night, and how
she vanished away.

Then Fergne went and spoke with Boann, Angus's
mother, and he told her all that had happened, and he bade
her to send and search all through Ireland if she could find a
young girl of the same appearance as the one Angus had seen
in his sleep. And then he left him in his mother's care, and she
had all Ireland searched for a year, but no young girl of that
appearance could be found.

At the end of the year, Boann sent for Fergne to come
again, and she said: "We have not got any help from our
search up to this." And Fergne said: "Send for the Dagda that

he may come and speak to his son." So they sent for the Dagda, and when he came, he said: "What have I been called for?" "To give an advice to your son," said Fergne, "and to help him, for he is lying sick on account of a young girl that appeared to him in his sleep, and that cannot be found; and it would be a pity for him to die." "What use will it be, I to speak to him?" said the Dagda, "for my knowledge is no higher than your own." "By my word," said Fergne, "you are the king of all the Sidhe of Ireland, and what you have to do is go to Bodb, the king of the Sidhe of Munster, for he has a name for knowledge all through Ireland." So messengers were sent to Bodb, at his house in Sidhe Femain, and he bade them welcome. "A welcome before you, messenger of the Dagda," he said, "and what is the message you have brought?" "This is the message," they said, "Angus Og, son of the Dagda, is wasting away these two years with love of a woman he saw in his dreams, and we have not been able to find her in any place. And this is an order to you," they said, "from the Dagda, to search out through Ireland a young girl of the same form and appearance as the one he saw." "The search will be made," said Bodb, "if it lasts me a year."

And at the end of a year he sent messengers to the Dagda. "Is it a good message you have brought?" said the Dagda. "It is, indeed," they said, "and this is the message Bodb bade us give you, 'I have searched all Ireland until I found the young girl with the same form and appearance that you said, at Loch Beul Draguin, at the Harp of Cliach.' And now," they said, "he bids Angus to come with us, till he sees if it is the same woman that appeared to him in his dream."

So Angus set out in his chariot to Sidhe Femain, and Bodb bade him welcome, and made a great feast for him, that lasted three days and three nights. And at the end of that time he said: "Come out now with me, and see if this is the same woman that came to you."

So they set out together till they came to the sea, and there they saw three times fifty young girls, and the one they were looking for among them; and she was far beyond them all. And there was a silver chain between every two of them, but about her own neck there was a necklace of shining gold. And Bodb said, "Do you see that woman you were looking for?" "I see her, indeed," said Angus. "But tell me who is she, and what her name is." Her name is Caer Ormaith, daughter of Ethal Anbual, from Sidhe Uaman, in the province of Connaught. But you cannot bring her away with you this time," said Bodb.

Then Angus went to visit his father, the Dagda, and his mother, Boann, at Brugh na Boinne; and Bodb went with him, and they told how they had seen the girl, and they had heard her own name, and her father's name. "What had we best do now?" said the Dagda. "The best thing for you to do," said

Bodb, "is to go to Ailell and Maeve, for it is in their district she lives, and you had best ask their help."

So the Dagda set out until he came into the province of Connaught, and sixty chariots with him; and Ailell and Maeve made a great feast for him. And after they had been feasting and drinking for the length of a week, Ailell asked the reason for their journey. And the Dagda said: "It is by reason of a young girl in your district, for my son has sickness upon him on account of her, and I am come to ask if you will give her to him." "Who is she?" said Ailell. "She is Caer Ormaith, daughter of Ethal Anbual." "We have no power over her that we could give her to him," said Ailell and Maeve. "The best thing for you to do," said the Dagda, "would be to call her father here to you."

So Ailell sent his steward to Ethal Anbual, and he said: "I am come to bid you to go and speak with Ailell and Maeve." "I will not go," he said; "I will not give my daughter to the son of the Dagda." So the steward went back and told this to Ailell. "He will not come," he said, "and he knows the reason you want him for."

Then there was anger on Ailell and on the Dagda, and they went out, and their armed men with them, and they destroyed the whole place of Ethal Anbual, and he was brought before them. And Ailell said to him: "Give your daughter now to the son of the Dagda." "That is what I cannot do," he said, "for there is a power over her that is greater than mine." "What power is that?" said Ailell. "It is an enchantment," he said, "that is on her, she to be in the shape of a bird for one year, and in her own shape the next year." "Which shape is on her at this time?" said Ailell. "I would not like to say that," said her father. "Your head from you if you will not tell it," said Ailell.

"Well," said he, "I will tell you this much; she will be in the shape of a swan next month at Loch Beul Draguin, and three fifties of beautiful birds will be along with her, and if you will go there, you will see her."

So then Ethal was set free, and he made friends again with Ailell and Maeve; and the Dagda went home and told Angus all that had happened, and he said; "Go next summer to Loch Beul Draguin, and call her to you there."

So when the time came, Angus Og went to the loch, and he saw the three times fifty white birds there, with their silver chains about their necks. And Angus stood in a man's shape at the edge of the loch, and he called to the girl: "Come and speak with me, O Caer!" "Who is calling me?" said Caer. "Angus calls you," he said, "and if you come, I swear by my word, I will not hinder you from going into the loch again." "I will come," she said. So she came to him, and he laid his two hands on her, and then, to hold to his word, he took the shape of a swan on himself, and they went into the loch together, and they went around it three times. And then they spread their wings and rose up from the loch, and went in that shape till they were at Brugh na Boinne. And as they were going, the music they made was so sweet that all the people that heard it fell asleep for three days and three nights.

And Caer stopped there with him ever afterwards, and from that time there was a friendship between Angus Og and Ailell and Maeve. And it was on account of that friendship, Angus gave them his help at the time of the war for the Brown Bull of Cuailgne.

The Coming of Finn

Lady Gregory

At the time Finn was born his father Cumhal, of the sons of Baiscne, Head of the Fianna of Ireland, had been killed in battle by the sons of Morna that were fighting with him for the leadership. And his mother, that was beautiful long-haired Muirne, daughter of Tadg, son of Nuada of the Tuatha de Danaan and of Ethlinn, mother of Lugh of the Long Hand, did not dare to keep him with her; and two women, Bodhmall, the woman Druid, and Liath Luachra, came and brought him away to care him.

It was to the woods of Slieve Bladhma they brought him, and they nursed him secretly, because of his father's enemies, the sons of Morna, and they kept him there a long time.

And Muirne, his mother, took another husband that was king of Carraighe; but at the end of six years she came to see Finn, going through every lonely place till she came to the wood, and there she found the little hunting cabin, and the boy asleep in it, and she lifted him up in her arms and kissed him, and she sang a little sleepy song to him; and then she said farewell to the women, and she went away again.

And the two women went on caring for him till he came to sensible years; and one day when he went out he saw a wild duck on the lake with her clutch, and he made a cast at her that cut the wings off her that she could not fly, and he brought her back to the cabin, and that was his first hunt.

And they gave him good training in running and leaping and swimming. One of them would run round a tree, and she having a thorn switch, and Finn after her with another switch, and each one trying to hit at the other; and they would leave him in a field, and hares along with him, and would bid him not to let the hares quit the field, but to keep before them whichever way they would go; and to teach him swimming they would throw him into the water and let him make his way out.

But after a while he went away with a troop of poets, to hide from the sons of Morna, and they hid him in the mountain of Crotta Cliach; but there was a robber in Leinster at that time, Fiacuil, son of Codhna, and he came where the poets were in Fidh Gaible and killed them all. But he spared the child and brought him to his own house, that was in a cold marsh. But the two women, Bodhmall and Liath, came looking for him after a while, and Fiacuil gave him up to them, and they brought him back to the same place he was before.

He grew up there, straight and strong and fair-haired and beautiful. And one day he was out in Slieve Bladhma, and the two women along with him, and they saw before them a herd of the wild deer of the mountain. "It is a pity," said the old women, "we not to be able to get a deer of those deer." "I will get one for you," said Finn; and with that he followed after them, and caught two stags of them and brought them home to the hunting cabin. And after that he used to be hunting for them every day. But at last they said to him: "It is best for you to leave us now, for the sons of Morna are watching again to kill you."

So he went away then by himself, and never stopped till he came to Magh Lifé, and there he saw young lads swimming in a lake, and they called to him to swim against them. So he went into the lake, and he beat them at swimming. "Fair he is and well shaped," they said when they saw him swimming, and it was from that time he got the name of Finn, that is, Fair. But they got to be jealous of his strength, and he went away and left them.

He went on then till he came to Loch Lein, and he took service there with the King of Finntraigh; and there was no hunter like him, and the king said: "If Cumhal had left a son, you would be that son."

He went from that king after, and he went into Carraighe and there he took service with the king that had taken his mother Muirne for his wife. And one day they were playing chess together, and he won seven games one after another. "Who are you at all?" said the king then. "I am a son of a countryman of the Luigne of Teamhair," said Finn. "That is not so," said the king, "but you are the son that Muirne my wife bore to Cumhal. And do not stop here any longer," he said, "that you may not be killed under my protection."

From that he went into Connacht looking for his father's brother Crimall, son of Trenmor; and as he was going on his way he heard the crying of a lone woman. He went to her, and looked at her, and tears of blood were on her face. "Your face is red with blood, woman," he said. "I have reason for it," said she, "for my only son is after being killed by a great fighting man that came on us." And Finn followed after the big champion and fought with him and killed him. And the man he killed was the same man that had given Cumhal his first wound in the battle where he got his death, and had brought away his treasure-bag with him.

Now as to that treasure-bag, it is of a crane skin it was made, that was one time the skin of Aoife, the beautiful sweetheart of Ilbrec, son of Manannan, that was put into the shape of a crane through jealousy. And it was in Manannan's house it used to be, and there were treasures kept in it, Manannan's shirt and his knife, and the belt and the smith's hook of Goibniu, and the shears of the King of Alban, and the helmet of the King of Lochlann, and a belt of the skin of a great fish, and the bones of Asal's pig that had been brought to Ireland by the sons of Tuireann. All those treasures would be in the bag at full tide, but at the ebbing of the tide it would be empty. And it went from Manannan to Lugh, son of Ethlinn, and after that to Cumhal, that was husband to Muirne, Ethlinn's daughter.

And Finn took the bag and brought it with him till he found Crimall, that was now an old man, living in a lonely place, and some of the old men of the Fianna were with him, and used to go hunting for him. And Finn gave him the bag, and told him his whole story.

And then he said farewell to Crimall, and went on to learn poetry from Finegas, a poet that was living at the Boinn, for the poets thought it was always on the brink of water poetry was revealed to them. And he did not give him his own name, but he took the name of Deimne. Seven years, now, Finegas had stopped at the Boinn, watching the salmon, for it was in the prophecy that he would eat the salmon of knowledge that would come there, and that he would have all knowledge after. And when at the last the salmon of knowledge came, he brought it to where Finn was, and bade him to roast it, but he bade him not to eat any of it. And when Finn brought him the salmon after a while he said: "Did you eat any of it at all, boy?" "I did not," said Finn; "but I burned my thumb putting down a blister that rose on the skin, and after doing that, I put my thumb in my mouth." "What is your name, boy?" said Finegas. "Deimne," said he. "It is not, but it is Finn your name is, and it is to you and not to myself the salmon was given in the prophecy." With that he gave Finn the whole of the salmon, and from that time Finn had the knowledge that came from the nuts of the nine hazels of wisdom that grow beside the well that is below the sea.

And besides the wisdom he got then, there was a second wisdom came to him another time, and this is the way it happened. There was a well of the moon belonging to Beag, son of Buan, of the Tuatha de Danaan, and whoever would drink out of it would get wisdom, and after a second drink he would get the gift of foretelling. And the three daughters of Beag, son of Buan, had charge of the well, and they would not part with a vessel of it for anything less than red gold. And one day Finn chanced to be hunting in the rushes near the well, and the three women ran out to hinder him from coming to it, and one of them had a vessel of the water in her hand, threw it at him to stop him, and a share of the water went into his mouth. And from that out he had all the knowledge that the water of the well could give.

And he learned the three ways of poetry; and this is the poem he made to show he had got his learning well:—

"It is the month of May is the pleasant time; its face is beautiful; the blackbird sings his full song, the living wood is his holding, the cuckoos are singing and ever singing; there is a welcome before the brightness of the summer.

"Summer is lessening the rivers, the swift horses are looking for the pool; the heath spreads out its long hair, the weak white bog-down grows. A wildness comes on the heart of the deer; the sad restless sea is asleep.

"Bees with their little strength carry a load reaped from the flowers; the cattle go up muddy to the mountains; the ant has a good full feast.

"The harp of the woods is playing music; there is colour on the hills, and a haze on the full lakes, and entire peace upon every sail.

"The corncrake is speaking, a loud-voiced poet; the high lonely waterfall is singing a welcome to the warm pool, the talking of the rushes has begun.

"The light swallows are darting; the loudness of music is around the hill; the fat soft mass is budding; there is grass on the trembling bogs.

"The bog is as dark as the feathers of the raven; the cuckoo makes a loud welcome; the speckled salmon is leaping; as strong as the leaping of the swift fighting man.

"The man is gaining; the girl is in her comely growing power; every wood is without fault from the top to the ground, and every wide good plain.

"It is pleasant is the colour of the time; rough winter is gone; every plentiful wood is white; summer is a joyful peace.

"A flock of birds pitches in the meadow; there are sounds in the green fields, there is in them a clear rushing stream.

"There is a hot desire on you for the racing of horses; twisted holly makes a leash for the hound; a bright spear has been shot into the earth, and the flag-flower is golden under it.

"A weak lasting little bird is singing at the top of his voice; the lark is singing clear tidings; May without fault, of beautiful colours.

"I have another story for you; the ox is lowing, the winter is creeping in, the summer is gone. High and cold the wind, low the sun, cries are about us; the sea is quarrelling.

"The ferns are reddened and their shape is hidden; the cry of the wild goose is heard; the cold has caught the wings of the birds; it is the time of ice-frost, hard, unhappy."

And after that, Finn being but a young lad yet, made himself ready and went up at Samhain time to the gathering of the High Kings at Teamhair. And it was the law at that gathering, no one to raise a quarrel or bring out any grudge against another through the whole of the time it lasted. And the king and his chief men, and Goll, son of Morna, that was now Head of the Fianna, and Caoilte, son of Ronan, and Conan, son of Morna, of the sharp words, were sitting at a feast in the great house of the Middle Court; and the young lad came in and took his place among them, and none of them knew who he was.

The High King looked at him then, and the horn of meetings was brought to him, and he put it into the boy's hand, and asked him who was he.

"I am Finn, son of Cumhal," he said, "son of the man that used to be head over the Fianna, and king of Ireland; and I am come now to get your friendship, and to give you my service."

"You are son of a friend, boy," said the king, "and son of a man I trusted."

Then Finn rose up and made his agreement of service and of faithfulness to the king; and the king took him by the hand and put him sitting beside his own son, and they gave themselves to drinking and to pleasure for a while.

Every year, now, at Samhain time, for nine years, there had come a man of the Tuatha de Danaan out of Sidhe Finnachaidh in the north, and has burned up Teamhair. Aillen, son of Midhna, his name was, and it is the way he used to come, playing music of the Sidhe, and all the people that heard

it would fall asleep. And when they were all in their sleep, he would let a flame of fire out of his mouth, and would blow the flame till all Teamhair was burned.

The king rose up at the feast after a while, and his smooth horn in his hand, and it is what he said: "If I could find among you, men of Ireland, any man that would keep Teamhair till the break of day to-morrow without being burned by Aillen, son of Midha, I would give him whatever inheritance is right for him to have, whether it be much or little."

But the men of Ireland made no answer, for they knew that at the sound of the sweet pitiful music made by that comely man of the Sidhe, even women in their pains and men that were wounded would fall asleep.

It is then Finn rose up and spoke to the King of Ireland. "Who will be your sureties that you will fulfil this?" he said. "The kings of the provinces of Ireland," said the king, "and Cithruadh with his Druids." So they gave their pledges, and Finn took in hand to keep Teamhair safe till the breaking of day on the morrow.

Now there was a fighting man among the followers of the King of Ireland, Fioacha, son of Cong, that Cumhal, Finn's father, used to have a great liking for, and he said to Finn: "Well, boy," he said, "what reward would you give me if I would bring you a deadly spear, that no false cast was ever made with?" "What reward are you asking of me?" said Finn.

"Whatever your right hand wins at any time, the third of it to be mine," said Fiacha, "and a third of your trust and your friendship to be mine." "I will give you that," said Finn. Then Fiacha brought him the spear, unknown to the sons of Morna or to any other person, and he said: "When you will hear the music of the Sidhe, let you strip the covering off the head of the spear and put it to your forehead, and the power of the spear will not let sleep come upon you."

Then Finn rose up before all the men of Ireland, and he made a round of the whole of Teamhair. And it was not long till he heard the sorrowful music, and he stripped the covering from the head of the spear, and he held the power of it to his forehead. And Aillen went on playing his little harp, till he had put every one in their sleep as he was used; and then he let a flame of fire out from his mouth to burn Teamhair. And Finn held up his fringed crimson cloak against the flame, and it fell down through the air and went into the ground, bringing the four-folded cloak with it deep into the earth.

And when Aillen saw his spells were destroyed, he went back to Sidhe Finnachaidh on the top of Slieve Fuad; but Finn followed after him there, and as Aillen was going in at the door he made a cast of the spear that went through his heart. And he struck his head off then, and brought it back to Teamhair, and fixed it on a crooked pole and left it there till the rising of the sun over the heights and invers of the country.

And Aillen's mother came to where his body was lying, and there was great grief on her, and she made this complaint:—

"Ochone! Aillen is fallen, chief of the Sidhe of Beinn Boirche; the slow clouds of death are come on him. Och! he was pleasant, Och! he was kind, Aillen, son of Midhna of Slieve Fuad.

"Nine times he burned Teamhair. It is a great name he was always looking for, Ochone, Ochone, Aillen!"

And at the breaking of day, the king and all the men of Ireland came out upon the lawn at Teamhair where Finn was. "King," said Finn, "there is the head of the man that burned Teamhair, and the pipe and the harp that made his music. And it is what I think," he said, "that Teamhair and all that is in it is saved."

Then they all came together into the place of counsel, and it is what they agreed, the headship of the Fianna of Ireland be given to Finn. And the king said to Goll, son of Morna: "Well, Goll," he said, "is it your choice to quit Ireland or to put your hand in Finn's hand?" "By my word, I will give Finn my hand," said Goll.

And when the charms that used to bring good luck had done their work, the chief men of the Fianna rose up and struck their hands in Finn's hand and Goll, son of Morna, was the first to give him his hand the way there would be less shame on the rest for doing it.

And Finn kept the headship of the Fianna until the end; and the place he lived in was Almhuin of Leinster, where the white dun was made by Nuada of the Tuatha de Danaan, that was as white as if all the lime in Ireland was put on it, and that got its name from the great heard of cattle that died fighting one time around the well, and that left their horns there, speckled horns and white.

And as to Finn himself, he was a king and a seer and a poet; a Druid and a knowledgeable man; and everything he said was sweet-sounding to his people. And a better fighting man than Finn never struck his hand into a king's hand, and whatever any one ever said of him, he was three times better. And of his justice it used to be said, that if his enemy and his own son had come before him to be judged, it is a fair judgment he would have given between them. And as to his generosity it used to be said, he never denied any man as long as he had a mouth to eat with, and legs to bring away what he gave him; and he left no woman without her bride-price, and no man without his pay; and he never promised at night what he would not fulfil on the morrow, and he never promised in the day what he would not fulfil at night, and he never forsook his right-hand friend. And if he was quiet in peace he was angry in battle, and Oisin his son and Osgar his son's son followed him in that. There was a young man of Ulster came and claimed kinship with them one time, saying they were of the one blood. "If that is so," said Oisin, "it is from the men of Ulster we took the madness and the angry heart we have in battle." "That is so indeed," said Finn.

Finn's House
Lady Gregory

And the number of the Fianna of Ireland at that time was seven score and ten chief men, every one of them having three times nine fighting men under him. And every man of them was bound to three things, to take no cattle by oppression, not to refuse any man, as to cattle or riches; no one of them to fall back before nine fighting men. And there was no man taken into the Fianna until his tribe and his kindred would give securities for him, that even if they themselves were all killed he would not look for satisfaction for their death. But if he himself would harm others, that harm was not to be avenged on his people. And there was no man taken into the Fianna till he knew the twelve books of poetry. And before any man was taken, he would be put into a deep hole in the ground up to his middle, and he having his shield and a hazel rod in his hand. And nine men would go the length of ten furrows from him and would cast their spears at him at the one time. And if he got a wound from one of them, he was not thought fit to join with the Fianna. And after that again, his hair would be fastened up, and he put to run through the woods of Ireland, and the Fianna following after him to try could they wound him, and only the length of a branch between themselves and himself when they started. And if they came up with him and wounded him, he was not let join them; or if his spears had trembled in his hand, or if a branch of a tree had undone the plaiting of his hair, or if he had cracked a dry stick under his foot, and he running. And they would not take him among them till he had made a leap over a stick the height of himself, and till he had stooped under one the height of his knee, and till he had taken a thorn out from his foot with his nail, and he running his fastest. But if he had done all these things, he was of Finn's people.

It was good wages Finn and the Fianna got at that time; in every district a townland, in every house the fostering of a pup or a whelp from Samhain to Beltaine, and a great many things along with that. But good as the pay was, the hardships and the dangers they went through for it were greater. For they had to hinder the strangers and robbers from beyond the seas, and every bad thing, from coming into

Ireland. And they had hard work enough in doing that.

And besides the fighting men, Finn had with him his five Druids, the best that ever came into the west, Cainnelsciath, of the Shining Shield, one of them was, that used to bring down knowledge from the clouds in the sky before Finn, and that could foretell battles. And he had his five wonderful physicians, four of them belonging to Ireland, and one that came over the sea from the east. And he had his five high poets and his twelve musicians, that had among them Daighre, son of Morna, and Suanach, son of Senshenn, that was Finn's teller of old stories, the sweetest that ever took a harp in his hand in Ireland or in Alban. And he had his three cup-bearers and his six door-keepers and his horn-players and the stewards of his house and his huntsman, Comhrag of the five hundred hounds, and his serving-men that were under Garbhcronan, of the Rough Buzzing; and a great troop of others along with them.

And there were fifty of the best sewing-women in Ireland brought together in a rath on Magh Feman, under the charge of a daughter of the King of Britain, and they used to be making clothing for the Fianna through the whole of the year. And three of them, that were a king's daughters, used to be making music for the rest on a little silver harp; and there was a very great candlestick of stone in the middle of the rath, for they were not willing to kindle a fire more than three times in the year for fear the smoke and the ashes might harm the needlework.

And of all his musicians the one Finn thought most of was Cru Deireoil, the Little Nut, that came to him from the Sidhe.

It was at Slieve-nam-ban, for hunting, Finn was the time he came to him. Sitting down he was on the turf-built grave that is there; and when he looked around him he saw a small little man about four feet in height standing on the grass. Light yellow hair he had, hanging down to his waist, and he playing music on his harp. And the music he was making had no fault in it at all, and it is much that the whole of the Fianna did not fall asleep with the sweetness of its sound. He came up then, and put his hand in Finn's hand, "Where do you come from, little one, yourself and your sweet music?" said Finn. "I am come," he said, "out of the place of the Sidhe in Slieve-nam-ban, where ale is drunk and made; and it is to be in your company for a while I am come here." "You will get good rewards from me, and riches and red gold," said Finn, "and my full friendship, for I like you well." "That is the best luck ever came to you, Finn," said all the rest of the Fianna, for they were well pleased to have him in their company. And they gave him the name of the Little Nut; and he was good in speaking, and he had so good a memory he never forgot anything he heard east or west; and there was no one but must listen to his music, and all the Fianna liked him well. And there were some said he was a son of Lugh Lamh-Fade, of the Long Hand.

And the five musicians of the Fianna were brought to him, to learn the music of the Sidhe he had brought from that other place; for there was never any music heard on earth but his was better. These were the three best things Finn ever got, Bran and Sceolan that were without fault, and the Little Nut from the House of the Sidhe in Slieve-nam-ban.

Diarmuid and Grania:
The Flight from Teamhair
Lady Gregory

Finn rose up one morning early in Almhuin of Leinster, and he sat out alone on the green lawn without a boy or a servant being with him. And Oisin followed him there, and Diorraing the Druid. "What is the cause of your early rising, Finn?" said Oisin. "It is not without cause, indeed, I rise early," said Finn, "for I am without a wife or a companion since Maighneis, daughter of Black Garraidh, died from me; for quiet sleep is not used to come to a man that is without a fitting wife." "Why would you be like that?" said Oisin, "for there is not a woman in all green Ireland you would throw a look on but we would bring her to you, willing or unwilling." "I myself could find a wife would be fitting for you," said

Diorraing. "Who is that?" said Finn. "It is Grania, daughter of the High King of Ireland," said Diorraing; "and she is the woman of the best make and shape and the best speech of the women of the whole world." "By my word, Diorraing," said Finn, "there is strife and disagreement between the High King and myself this long time, and it would not be pleasing to me to get a refusal from him. And it is best for you two to go together," he said, "and to ask his daughter for me in marriage; the way that if he gives a refusal, it will be to you and not to myself he will give it." "We will go," said Oisin, "even if it is little profit we will get by it. And let no one at all know of our going," he said, "until such time as we are come back again."

After that the two bade farewell to Finn, and set out, and it is not told what they did till they came to Teamhair. The King of Ireland was holding a gathering at that time on the green of Teamhair, and the chief nobles of his people were with him. And there was a friendly welcome given to Oisin and to Diorraing, and the king put off the gathering till the next day, for he was sure it was some pressing thing had brought these two men of the Fianna to Teamhair. And Oisin went aside with him, and told him it was to ask his daughter Grania in marriage they were come from Finn, Head of the Fianna of Ireland.

The king spoke, and it is what he said: "There is not a son of a king or of a great prince, there is not a champion in

Ireland my daughter has not given a refusal to, and it is on me they all lay the blame of that. And I will give you no answer at all," he said, "till you go to herself; for it is better for you to get her own answer, than to be displeased with me." So they went together to the sunny house of the women, and the king sat down at the head of the high seat beside Grania, and he said: "Here, Grania, are two of the people of Finn, son of Cumhal, come to ask you as a wife for him, and what answer have you a mind to give them?" And it was what Grania said: "If he is a fitting son-in-law for you, why would he not be a fitting husband for me?"

They were satisfied then, and there was a feast made for them that night in Grania's sunny house, and the king settled for a meeting a fortnight from that time between himself and Finn at Teamhair.

So Oisin and Diorraing went back again to Almhuin, and told Finn their story from beginning to end. And as everything wears away, so did that time of delay.

And then Finn gathered together the seven battalions of the Fianna from every part where they were to Almhuin. And they set out in great bands and troops till they came to Teamhair.

The king was out on the green before them, and the great people of the men of Ireland, and there was a great welcome before Finn and the Fianna.

But when Grania saw grey-haired Finn, she said: "It is a great wonder it was not for Oisin Finn asked me, for he would be more fitting for me than a man that is older than my father."

But they talked together for a while, and Finn was putting questions to Grania, for she had the name of being very quick with answers. "What is whiter than snow?" he said. "The truth," said Grania. "What is the best colour?" said Finn. "The colour of childhood," said she. "What is hotter than fire?" "The face of a hospitable man when he sees a stranger coming in, and the house empty." "What has a taste more bitter than poison?" "The reproach of an enemy." "What is best for a champion?" "His doings to be high, and his pride to be low." "What is the best of jewels?" "A knife." "What is sharper than a sword?" "The wit of a woman between two men." "What is quicker than the wind?" said Finn then. "A woman's mind," said Grania. And indeed she was telling no lie when she said that. And for all their talk together she had no liking for Finn, and she felt the blood in her heart to be rising against him.

And the wedding-feast was made ready then, and they all went into the king's feasting-house in the Middle Court. And the king sat down to take his share of drinking and pleasure, and his wife at his left side, and Grania beside her again; and Finn, son of Cumhal, at the right hand of the king, and Oisin at the other side, and every other one according to his nobility and his birth.

Then Daire of the poems stood up before Grania, and sang the songs and good poems of her fathers to her. And there was sitting near to Grania a knowledgable man, a Druid of Finn's people, and it was not long until they began to talk together. "Tell me now," said Grania, "who is that man on the right hand of Oisin?" "That is Goll, son of Morna," said the Druid, "the ready fighter." "Who is that beside Goll?" said Grania. "Osgar, son of Oisin," said the Druid. "And who is that thin-legged man beside Osgar?" "That is Caoilte, son of Ronan." "Who is that proud, hasty man beside Caoilte?" "Lugaidh's Son of the Strong Hand." "Who is that sweet-worded man," she said then, "with the dark hair, and cheeks like the rowan berry, on the left side of Oisin, son of Finn?" "That is Diarmuid, grandson of Duibhne," said the Druid, "that is the best lover of women in the whole world." "That is a good company," said Grania.

And after the feast had gone on a while, their own feast was made for the dogs outside. And the dogs began to fight with one another, and the noise was heard in the hall, and the chief men of the Fianna went to drive them away from one another.

Now Diarmuid was used to keep his cap always over the love-spot the woman had left on his forehead, for no woman could see that spot but she would give him her love. And it chanced, while he was driving the dogs apart, the cap fell from him, and Grania was looking out at him as it fell, and great love for him came on her there and then. And she called her serving-maid to her, and bade her bring the great golden cup that held drink for nine times nine men from the sunny house. And when the serving-maid brought the cup, she filled it with wine that had enchantment in it, and she said: "Give the cup first to Finn, and bid him take a drink from it, and tell him it is I myself sent it to him." So the serving-maid did that, and Finn took the cup and drank out of it, and no sooner did he drink than he fell into a deep sleep. And then the cup was given to the king, and the queen, and the sons of kings, and the whole company, but only Oisin and Osgar and Caoilte and Diarmuid, and Diorraing the Druid. And all that drank of it fell into the same heavy sleep.

And when they were all in their sleep, Grania rose up softly from the seat where she was, and she turned her face to Diarmuid, and she said: "Will you take my love, Diarmuid, son of Duibhne, and will you bring me away out of this house to-night?"

"I will not," said Diarmuid; "I will not meddle with the woman that is promised to Finn." "If that is so," said Grania, "I put you under Druid bonds, to bring me out of this house to-night before the awaking of Finn and the King of Ireland from their sleep."

"It is under bad bonds you are putting me, Grania," said Diarmuid. "And why is it," he said, "that you put them on me more than on the great men and sons of kings that are in the Middle Court to-night? for there is not one of them all but is well worthy of a woman's love as myself." "By my hand, Diarmuid, it is not without cause I laid those bonds on you," said Grania; "for I was at the door a while ago when you were parting the dogs," she said, "and my eyes fell on you, and I gave you the love there and then that I never gave to any other, and never will give for ever."

"It is a wonder you to give that love to me, and not to Finn," said Diarmuid, "for there is not in Ireland a man is a better lover of a woman than himself. And do you know this, Grania," he said, "the night Finn is in Teamhair it is he himself is the keeper of its gates. And as that is so, we cannot leave the town." "There is a side door of escape at my sunny house," said Grania, "and we will go out by it." "It is a thing I will never do," said Diarmuid, "to go out by any side door of escape at all." "That may be so," said Grania, "but I heard it said that every fighting man has leave to pass over the walls of any dun and of any strong place at all by the shafts of his spears. And I will go out through the door," she said, "and let you follow me like that."

With that she went out, and Diarmuid spoke to his people, and it is what he said, "O Oisin, son of Finn, what must I do with these bonds that are laid on me?" "You are not guilty if the bonds were laid on you," said Oisin; "and I tell you to follow Grania, and to keep yourself well out of the hands of Finn." "Osgar, son of Oisin," he said then, "what must I do with these bonds that are put on me?" "I tell you to follow Grania," said Osgar, "for it is a pitiful man that would break his bonds." "What advice do you give me, Caoilte?" said Diarmuid. "It is what I say," said Caoilte, "that I myself have a fitting wife; and that it would be better to me than all the riches of the world Grania to have given me that love." "What advice do you give me, Diorraing?" "I tell you to follow Grania," said Diorraing, "although you will get your death by it, and that is bad to me." "Is that the advice you all give me?" said Diarmuid. "It is," said Oisin, and all the rest with him. With that Diarmuid stood up and stretched out his hand for his weapons, and he said farewell to Oisin and the others, and every tear he shed was of the size of a mountain berry. He went out then to the wall of the dun, and he put the shafts of his two spears under him, and he rose with a light leap and he came down on the grassy earth outside, and Grania met him there. Then Diarmuid said: "It is a bad journey you are come on, Grania. For it would be better for you to have Finn, son of Cumhal, as a lover than myself, for I do not know any part or any western corner of Ireland that will hide you. And if I do bring you with me," he said, "it is not as a wife I will bring you, but I will keep my faith to Finn. And turn back now to the town," he said, "and Finn will never get news of what you

are after doing." "It is certain I will not turn back," said
Grania, "and I will never part with you till death parts us."
"If that is so, let us go on, Grania," said Diarmuid.

They went on then, and they were not gone far out
from the town when Grania said: "I am getting tired, indeed."
"It is a good time to be tired," said Diarmuid, "and go now back
again to your own house. For I swear by the word of a true
champion," he said, "I will never carry yourself or any other
woman to the end of life and time." "That is not what you have
to do,"said Grania, "for my father's horses are in a grass field
by themselves, and chariots with them; and turn back now,
and bring two horses of them, and I will wait in this place till
you come to me again."

Diarmuid went back then for the horses, and we have
no knowledge of their journey till they reached to the ford on
the Sionnan, that is called now Ath-luain.

And Diarmuid said then to Grania: "It is easier to Finn
to follow our track, the horses being with us." "If that is so,"
said Grania: "leave the horses here, and I will go on foot
from this out."

Diarmuid went down to the river then, and he brought
a horse with him over the ford, and left the other horse the far
side of the river. And he himself and Grania went a good way
with the stream westward, and they went to land at the side
of the province of Connacht. And wherever they went,

Diarmuid left unbroken bread after him, as a sign to Finn he had kept his faith with him.

And from that they went on to Doire-da-Bhoth, the Wood of the Two Huts. And Diarmuid cut down the wood round about them, and he made a fence having seven doors of woven twigs, and he set out a bed of soft rushes and of the tops of the birch-tree for Grania in the very middle of the wood.

Diarmuid and Grania: The Pursuit

Lady Gregory

And as to Finn, son of Cumhal, I will tell out his story now.

All that were in Teamhair rose up early in the morning of the morrow, and they found Diarmuid and Grania were wanting from them, and there came a scorching jealousy and a weakness on Finn. He sent out his trackers then on the plain, and bade them to follow Diarmuid and Grania. And they followed the track as far as the ford on the Sionnan, and Finn and the Fianna followed after them, but they were not able to carry the track across the ford. And Finn gave them his word that unless they would find the track again without delay, he would hang them on each side of the ford.

Then the sons of Neamhuin went up against the

stream, and they found a horse on each side of it, and then they went on with the stream westward, and they found the track going along the side of the Province of Connacht, and Finn and the Fianna of Ireland followed it on. And Finn said: "I know well where we will find Diarmuid and Grania now; it is in Doire-da-Bhoth they are." Oisin and Osgar and Caoilte and Diorraing were listening when Finn said those words. And Osgar spoke to the others, and it is what he said: "There is danger they might be there, and it would be right for us to give them some warning; and look now, Osgar, where is Bran thee hound, for Finn himself is no dearer to him than Diarmuid, and bid him go now with a warning to him."

So Osgar told Bran, and Bran understood him well, and she went to the rear of the whole troop the way Finn would not see her, and she followed on the track of Diarmuid and Grania till she came to Doire-da-Bhoth, and she put her head into Diarmuid's bosom, and he in his sleep.

Diarmuid started up out of his sleep then, and he awoke Grania, and said to her: "Here is Bran, Finn's hound, and she is come with a warning to tell us Finn himself is coming." "Let us take that warning, then," said Grania, "and make your escape." "I will not take it," said Diarmuid, "for if I cannot escape Finn, I would as soon he took me now as at any other time." When Grania heard that, great fear came on her.

Bran went away from them then, and when Oisin saw

her coming back, he said: "I am in dread Bran found no chance to get to Diarmuid, and we should send him some other warning. And look where is Fearghoin," he said, "Caoilte's serving-man." Now it was the way with Fearghoin, every shout he would give would be heard in the three nearest hundreds to him. So they made him give out three shouts the way Diarmuid would hear him. And Diarmuid heard him, and he said to Grania: "I hear Caoilte's serving-man, and it is with Caoilte he is, and it is along with Finn Caoilte is, and those shouts were sent as a warning to me." "Take that warning," said Grania. "I will not take it," said Diarmuid, "for Finn and the Fianna will come up with us before we leave the wood." And fear and great dread came on Grania when she heard him say that.

As for Finn, he did not leave off following the track till he came to Doire-da-Bhoth, and he sent the sons of Neamhuin to search through the wood, and they saw Diarmuid, and the woman along with him. They came back then where Finn was, and he asked them were Diarmuid and Grania in the wood? "Diarmuid is in it," they said, "and there is some woman with him, but we knew Diarmuid, and we do not know Grania." "May no good come to the friends of Diarmuid for his sake," said Finn, "and he will not quit that wood till he has given me satisfaction for everything he has done to me."

"It is jealousy has put you astray, Finn," said Oisin; "you

to think Diarmuid would stop here on the plain of Maen Mhagh, and no close place in it but Doire-da-Bhoth, and you following after him." "Saying that will do you no good, said Finn, "for I knew well when I heard the three shouts Caoilte's serving-man gave out, it was you sent them to Diarmuid as a warning. And another thing," he said, "it was you sent my own hound Bran to him. But none of those things you have done will serve you, for he will not leave Doire-da-Bhoth till he gives me satisfaction for everything he has done to me, and every disgrace he has put on me." "It is great foolishness for you, Finn," said Osgar then, "to be thinking Diarmuid would stop in the middle of this plain and you waiting here to strike the head off him." "Who but himself cut the wood this way," said Finn, "and made this close sheltered place with seven woven narrow doors to it. And O Diarmuid," he said out then, "which of us is the truth with, myself or Oisin?" "You never failed from your good judgment, Finn," said Diarmuid, "and indeed I myself and Grania are here." Then Finn called to his men to go around Diarmuid and Grania, and to take them.

Now it was shown at this time to Angus Og, at Brugh na Boinne, the great danger Diarmuid was in, that was his pupil at one time, and his dear foster-son. He set out then with the clear cold wind, and did not stop in any place till he came to Doire-da-Bhoth. And he went unknown to Finn or the

Fianna into the place where Diarmuid and Grania were, and he spoke kind words to Diarmuid, and he said: "What is the thing you have done, grandson of Duibhne?" "It is," said Diarmuid, "the daughter of the King of Ireland that has made her escape with me from her father and from Finn, and it is not by my will she came." "Let each of you come under a border of my cloak, so," said Angus, "and I will bring you out of the place where you are without knowledge of Finn or his people." "Bring Grania with you," said Diarmuid, "but I will never go with you; but if I am alive I will follow you before long. And if I do not," he said, "give Grania to her father, and he will do well or ill to her."

With that Angus put Grania under the border of his cloak, and brought her out unknown to Finn or the Fianna, and there is no news told of them till they came to Ros-da-Shoileach, the Headland of the Two Sallows.

And as to Diarmuid, after Angus and Grania going from him, he stood up as straight as a pillar and put on his armour and his arms, and after that he went to a door of the seven doors he had made, and he asked who was at it. "There is no enemy to you here," they said, "for there are here Oisin and Osgar and the best men of the sons of Baiscne along with us. And come out to us now, and no one will have the daring to do any harm or hurt on you." "I will not go out to you," said Diarmuid, "till I see at what door Finn himself is." He went then to another door of the seven and asked who was at it. "Caoilte, son of Ronan, and the rest of the sons of Ronan along with him; and come out to us now, and we will give ourselves for your sake." "I will not go out to you," said Diarmuid, "for I will not put you under Finn's anger for any well-doing to myself." He went on to another door then and asked who was at it. "There is Conan, son of Morna, and the rest of the sons of Morna along with him; and it is enemies to Finn we are, and you are a great deal more to us than he is, and you may come out and no one will dare lay a hand on you." "I will not indeed," said Diarmuid, "for Finn would be better pleased to see the death of every one of you than to let me escape." He went then to another door and asked who was at it. "A friend and a comrade of your own, Fionn, son of Cuadan, head of the Fianna of Munster, and his men along with him; and we are of the one country and the one soil, and we will give our bodies and our lives for your sake." "I will not go out to you," said Diarmuid, "for I would not like Finn to have a grudge against you for any good you did to me." He went then to another door and asked who was at it. "It is Fionn, son of Glor, head of the Fianna of Ulster, and his men along with him; and come out now to us and there is no one will dare hurt or harm you." "I will not go out to you," said Diarmuid, "for you are a friend to me, and your father along with you, and I would not like the unfriendliness of Finn to be put on you for my sake." He went then to another door, and he asked who was at it. "There is no friend of yours here," they said, "for there is here Aodh Beag the Little from Eamhuin, and Aodh Fada the Long from Eamhuin, and Caol Crodha the Fierce, and Goineach the Wounder, and Gothan the White-fingered, and Aoife his daughter, and Cuadan the Tracker from Eamhuin; and we are unfriendly people to you, and if you come out to us we will not spare you at all, but will make an end of you." "It is a bad troop is in it," said Diarmuid; "you of the lies and of the tracking and of the one shoe, and it is not fear of your hands is upon me, but because I am your enemy I will not go out."

He went then to the last of the seven doors and asked who was at it. "No friend of yours," they said, "but it is Finn, son of Cumhal, and four hundred paid fighting men along with him; and if you will come out to us we will make opened marrow of you." "I give you my word, Finn," said Diarmuid, "that the door you are at yourself is the first door I will pass out of."

When Finn heard that, he warned his battalions on pain of lasting death not to let Diarmuid past them unknown. But when Diarmuid heard what he said, he rose on the staves of his spears and he went with a very high, light leap on far beyond Finn and his people, without their knowledge. He looked back at them then, and called out that he had gone past them, and he put his shield on his back and went straight on towards the west, and it was not long before he was out of sight of Finn and the Fianna. Then when he did not see any one coming after him, he turned back to where he saw Angus and Grania going out of the wood, and he followed on their track till he came to Ros-da-Shoileach.

He found Angus and Grania there in a sheltered, well-lighted cabin, and a great blazing fire kindled in it, and the half of a wild boar on spits. Diarmuid greeted them, and the life of Grania all to went out of her with joy before him.

Diarmuid told them his news from beginning to end, and they ate their share that night, and they went to sleep till the coming of the day and of the full light on the morrow. And Angus rose up early, and he said to Diarmuid: "I am going from you now, grandson of Duibhne; and I leave this advice with you," he said, "not to go into a tree with one trunk, and you flying before Finn, and not to be going into a cave of the earth that has but one door, and not to be going to an island of the sea that has but one harbour. And in whatever place you cook your share of food," he said, "do not eat it there; and in whatever place you eat it, do not lie down there; and in whatever place you lie down, do not rise up there on the morrow." He said farewell to them after that, and went his way.

Birth of Cuchulain

Lady Gregory

In the time long ago, Conchubar, son of Ness, was King of Ulster, and he held his court in the palace of Emain Macha. And this is the way he came to be king. He was but a young lad, and his father was not living, and Fergus, son of Rogh, who was at that time King of Ulster, asked his mother Ness in marriage.

Now Ness, that was at one time the quietest and kindest of the women of Ireland, had got to be unkind and treacherous because of an unkindness that had been done to her, and she planned to get the kingdom away from Fergus for her own son. So she said to Fergus: "Let Concubar hold the kingdom for a year, so that his children after him may be called the children of a king; and that is the marriage portion I will ask of you."

"You may do that," the men of Ulster said to him; "for even though Conchubar gets the name of being king it is yourself that will be our king all the time." So Fergus agreed to it, and he took Ness as his wife, and her son Conchubar was made king in his place.

But all through the year, Ness was working to keep the kingdom for him, and she gave great presents to the chief men of Ulster to get them on her side. And though Concubar was but a young lad at that time, he was wise in his judgments, and brave in battle, and good in shape and in form, and they liked him well. And at the end of the year, when Fergus asked to have the kingship back again, they consulted together; and it is what they agreed, that Conchubar was to keep it. And they said: "It is little Fergus thinks about us, when he was so ready to give up his rule over us for a year; and let Conchubar keep the kingship," they said, "and let Fergus keep the wife he has got."

Now it happened one day that Conchubar was making a feast at Emain Macha for the marriage of his sister Dechtire with Sualtim son of Roig. And at the feast Dechtire was thirsty, and they gave her a cup of wine, and as she was drinking it, a mayfly flew into the cup, and she drank it down with the wine. And presently she went into her sunny parlour, and her fifty maidens along with her, and she fell into a deep sleep. And in her sleep, Lugh of the Long Hand appeared to her, and he said: "It is myself was the mayfly that came to you in the cup, and it is with me you must come away now, and your fifty maidens along with you." And he put on them the appearance of a flock of birds, and they went with him southward till they came to Brugh na Boinne, the dwelling-place of the Sidhe. And no one at Emain Macha could get tale or tidings of them, or know where they had gone, or what had happened to them.

It was about a year after that time, there was another feast in Emain, and Conchubar and his chief men were sitting at the feast. And suddenly they saw from the window a great flock of birds that lit on the ground, and began to eat up everything before them, so that not as much as a blade of grass was left.

The men of Ulster were vexed when they saw the birds destroying all before them, and they yoked nine of their chariots to follow after them. Conchubar was in his own chariot, and here were following with him Fergus son of Rogh, and Laegaire Buadach, the Battle-Winner, and Celthair son of Uithecar, and many others, and Bricriu of the bitter tongue was along with them.

They followed after the birds across the whole country southward, across Slieve Fuad, by Ath Lethan, by Ath Garach and Magh Gossa, between Fir Rois and Fir Ardae; and the birds before them always. They were the most beautiful that had ever been seen; nine flocks of them there were, linked together two and two with a chain of silver, and at the head of every flock there were two birds of different colours, linked together with a chain of gold; and there were three birds that flew by themselves, and they all went before the chariots, to the far end of the country, until the fall of night, and then there was no more seen of them.

And when the dark night was coming on, Conchubar said to his people: "It is best for us to unyoke the chariots now, and to look for some place where we can spend the night."

Then Fergus went forward to look for some place, and what he came to was a very small poor-looking house. A man and a woman were in it, and when they saw him they said: "Bring your companions here along with you, and they will be welcome." Fergus went back to his companions and told them what he had seen. But Bricriu said: "Where is the use of going into a house like that, with neither room nor provisions nor coverings in it; it is not worth our while to be going there."

Then Bricriu went on himself to the place where the house was. But when he came to it, what he saw was a grand, new, well-lighted house; and at the door there was a young man wearing armour, very tall and handsome and shining. And he said: "Come into the house, Bricriu; why are you looking about you?" And there was a young woman beside him, fine and noble, and with curled hair, and she said: "Surely there is a welcome before you from me." "Why does she welcome me?" said Bricriu. "It is on account of her that I myself welcome you," said the young man. "And there is no one missing from you at Emain?" he said. "There is surely, " said Bricriu. "We are missing fifty young girls for the length of a year." "Would you know them again if you saw them?" said the young man. "If I would not know them," said Bricriu, "it is because a year might make a change in them, so that I would not be sure." "Try and know them again," said the man, "for fifty young girls are in this house, and this woman beside me is their mistress, Dechtire. It was they themselves, changed into birds, that went to Emain Macha to bring you here." Then Dechtire gave Bricriu a purple cloak with gold fringes; and he went back to find his companions. But while he was going he thought to himself: "Conchubar would give great treasure to find these fifty young girls again, and his sister along with them. I will not tell him I have found them. I will only say I have found a house with beautiful women in it, and no more than that."

When Conchubar saw Bricriu, he asked news of him. "What news do you bring back with you, Bricriu?" he said. "I came to a fine well-lighted house," said Bricriu; "I saw a queen, noble, kind, with royal looks, with curled hair; I saw a troop of women, beautiful, well-dressed; I saw the man of the house, tall and open-handed and shining." "Let us go there for the night," said Conchubar. So they brought their chariots and their horses and their arms; and they were hardly in the house when every sort of food and of drink, some they knew and some they did not know, was put before them, so that they never spent a better night. And when they had eaten and drunk and began to be satisfied, Conchubar said to the young man: "Where is the mistress of the house that she does not come to bid us welcome?" "You cannot see her tonight for she is in the pains of childbirth."

So they rested there that night, and in the morning Conchubar was the first to rise up; but he saw no more of the man of the house, and what he heard was the cry of a child. And he went to the room it came from, and there he saw Dechtire, and her maidens about her, and a young child beside her. And she bade Conchubar welcome, and she told him all that had happened her, and that she had called him there to bring herself and the child back to Emain Macha. And Conchubar said: "It is well you have done by me, Dechtire; you gave shelter to me and to my chariots; you kept the cold from my horses; you gave food to me and my people, and now, you have given us this good gift. And let our sister, Finchoem, bring up the child," he said. "No, it is not for her to bring him up, it is for me," said Sencha son of Ailell, chief judge and chief poet of Ulster. "For I am skilled; I am good in disputes, I am not forgetful; I speak before any one at all in the presence of the king; I watch over what he says; I give judgment in the quarrel of kings; I am a judge of the men of Ulster; no one has a right to dispute my claim, but only Conchubar."

"If the child is given to me to bring up," said Blai, the distributer, "he will not suffer from want of care or from forgetfulness. It is my messages that do the will of Conchubar; I call up the fighting men from all Ireland. I am well able to provide for them for a week, or even for ten days; I settle their business and their disputes; I support their honour; I get satisfaction for their insults."

"You think too much of yourself," said Fergus. "It is I that will bring up the child; I am strong; I have knowledge; I am the king's messenger; no one can stand up against me in honour or riches; I am hardened to war and battles; I am a good craftsman; I am worthy to bring up a child. I am the protector of all the unhappy; the strong are afraid of me; I am the helper of the weak."

"If you will listen to me at last, now you are quiet," said Amergin, "I am able to bring up a child like a king. The people praise my honour, my bravery, my courage, my wisdom; they praise my good luck, my age, my speaking, my name, my courage, and my race. Though I am a fighter, I am a poet, I am worthy of the king's favour; I overcome all the men who fight from their chariots; I owe thanks to no one except Conchubar; I obey no one but the king."

Then Sencha said: "Let Finchoem keep the child until we come to Emain, and Morann, the judge, will settle the question when we are there."

So the men of Ulster set out for Emain, Finchoem having the child with her. And when they came there Morann gave his judgment. "It is for Conchubar," he said, "to help the child to a good name, for he is next of kin to him; let Sencha teach him words and speaking; let Fergus hold him on his knees; let Amergin be his tutor." And he said: "This child shall be praised by all, by chariot drivers and fighters, by kings and by wise men; he shall be loved by many men; he will avenge all your wrongs; he will defend your fords; he will fight all your battles."

And so it was settled. And the child left until he should come to sensible years, with his mother Dechtire and with her husband Sualtim. And they brought him up upon the plain of Muirthemne, and the name he was known by was Sentanta, son of Sualtim.

Boy Deeds of Cuchulain

Lady Gregory

It chanced one day, when Setanta was about seven years old, that he heard some of the people of his mother's house talking about King Conchubar's court at Emain Macha, and of the sons of kings and nobles that lived there, and that spent a great part of their time at games and at hurling. "Let me go and play with them there," he said to his mother. "It is too soon for you to do that," she said, "but wait till such time as you are able to travel so far, and till I can put you in charge of some one going to the court, that will put you under Conchubar's protection." "It would be too long for me to wait for that," he said, "but I will go there by myself if you will tell me the road." "It is too far for you," said Dichtire, "for it is beyond Slieve Fuad, Emain Macha is." "Is it east or west of Slieve Fuad?" he asked. And when she had answered him that, he set out there and then, and nothing with him but his hurling stick, and his silver ball, and his little dart and spear; and to shorten the road for himself he would give a blow to the ball and drive it from him, and then he would throw his hurling stick after it, and the dart after that again, and then he would make a run and catch them all in his hand before one of them would have reached the ground.

So he went on until he came to the lawn at Emain Macha, and there he saw three fifties of king's sons hurling, and learning feats of war. He went in among them, and when the ball came near him he got it between his feet, and drove it along in spite of them till he had sent it beyond the goal. There was great surprise and anger on them when they saw what he had done, and Follaman, King Conchubar's son, that was chief among them, cried out to them to come together and drive out this stranger and make an end of him. "For he has no right," he said, "to come into our game without asking leave, and without putting his life under our protection. And you may be sure," he said, "that he is the son of some common fighting man, and it is not for him to come into our game at all." With that they all made an attack on him, and began to throw their hurling sticks at him, and their balls and darts, but he escaped them all, and then he rushed at them, and began to throw some of them to the ground. Fergus came out just then from the palace, and when he saw what a good defence the little lad was making, he brought him in to where Conchubar was playing chess, and told him all that had happened. "This is no gentle game you have been playing," he said. "It is on themselves the fault is," said the boy; "I came as a stranger, and I did not get a stranger's welcome." "You did not know then," said Conchubar, "that no one can play among the boys of Emain unless he gets their leave and their protection." "I did not know that, or I would have asked it of them," he said. "What is your name and your family?" said Conchubar. "My name is Setanta, son of Sualtim and of Dechtire," he said. When Conchubar knew that he was his sister's son, he gave him a great welcome, and he bade the boy troop to let him go safe among them. "We will do that," they said. But when they went out to play, Setanta began to break through them, and to overthrow them, so that they could not stand against him. "What are you wanting of them now?" said Conchubar. "I swear by the gods my people swear by," said the boy, "I will not lighten my hand off them till they have come under my protection the same way I have come under theirs." Then they all agreed to give in to this, and Setanta stayed in the king's house at Emain Macha, and all the chief men of Ulster had a hand in bringing him up.

There was a great smith in Ulster of the name of

Culain, who made a feast at that time for Conchubar and for his people. When Conchubar was setting out to the feast, he passed the lawn where the boy troop were at their game, and he watched them awhile, and he saw how the son of Dechtire was winning the goal from them all. "That little lad will serve Ulster yet," said Conchubar; "and call him to me now," he said, "and let him come with me to the smith's feast." "I cannot go with you now," said Setanta, when they had called to him, "for these boys have not had enough of play yet." "It would be too long for me to wait for you," said the king. "There is no need for you to wait; I will follow the track of your chariots," said Setanta.

So Conchubar went on to the smith's house, and there was a welcome before him, and fresh rushes were laid down, and there were poems and songs and recitals of laws, and the feast was brought in, and they began to be merry. And then Culain said to the king: "Will there be any one else of your people coming after you tonight?" "There will not," said Conchubar, for he forgot that he had told the little lad to follow him. "But why do you ask me that?" he said. "I have a great fierce hound," said the smith, "and when I take the chain off him, he lets no one come into the one district with himself, and he will obey no one but myself, and he has in him the strength of a hundred." "Loose him out," said Conchubar, "until he keeps watch on the place." So Culain loosed him out, and the dog made a course round the whole district, and then he came back to the place where he was used to lie and to watch the house, and every one was in dread of him, he was so fierce and so cruel and so savage.

Now, as to the boys at Emain, when they were done playing, every one went to his father's house, or to whoever was in charge of him. But Setanta set out on the track of the chariots, shortening the way for himself as he was used to do with his hurling stick and his ball. When he came to the lawn before the smith's house, the hound heard him coming, and began such a feirce yelling that he might have been heard through all Ulster, and he sprang at him as if he had a mind not to stop and tear him up at all, but to swallow him at the one mouthful. The little fellow had no weapon but his stick and his ball, but when he saw the hound coming at him, he struck the ball with such force that it went down his throat, and through his body. Then he seized him by the hind legs and dashed him against a rock until there was no life left in him.

When the feasting men within heard the outcry of the hound, Conchubar started up and said: "It is no good luck brought us on this journey, for that is surely my sister's son that was coming after me, and that has got his death by the hound." On that all the men rushed out, not waiting to go through the doors, but over walls and barriers as they could. But Fergus was the first to get to where the boy was, and he took him up and lifted him on his shoulder, and brought him in safe and sound to Conchubar, and there was great joy on them all.

But Culain the smith went out with them, and when he saw his great hound lying dead and broken there was great grief in his heart, and he came in and said to Setanta: "There is no good welcome for you here." "What have you against the little lad?" said Conchubar. "It was no good luck that brought him here, or that made me prepare this feast for yourself, King," he said; "for from this out, my hound being gone, my substance will be wasted, and my way of living will be gone astray. And, little boy," he said "that was a good member of my family you took from me, for he was the protector of my goods and my flocks and my herds and of all that I had." "Do not be vexed on account of that," said the boy, "and I myself will make up to you for what I have done." "How will you do that?" said Conchubar. "This is how I will do it: if there is a whelp of the same breed to be had in Ireland, I will rear him and train him until he is as good a hound as the one killed; and until that time, Culain," he said, "I myself will be your watch-dog, to guard your goods and your cattle and your house." "You have made a fair offer," said Conchubar. "I could have given no better award myself," said Cathbad the Druid. "And from this day out," he said, "your name shall be

Cuchulain, the Hound of Culain." "I am better pleased with my own name of Setanta, son of Sualtim," said the boy. "Do not say that," said Cathbad, "for all men in the whole world will some day have the name of Cuchulain in their mouths." "If that is so, I am content to keep it," said the boy. And this is how he came by the name Cuchulain.

The Courting of Emer
Lady Gregory

When Cuchulain was growing out of his boyhood at Emain Macha, all the women of Ulster loved him for his skill in feats, for the lightness of his leap, for the weight of his wisdom, for the sweetness of his speech, for the beauty of his face, for the loveliness of his looks, for all his gifts. He had the gift of caution in fighting, until such time as his anger would come on him, and the hero light would shine about his head; the gift of feats, the gift of chess-playing, the gift of draught-playing, the gift of counting, the gift of divining, the gift of right judgment, the gift of beauty. And all the faults they could find in him were three, that he was too young and smooth-faced, so that young men who did not know him would be laughing at him, that he was too daring, and that he was too beautiful.

The men of Ulster took counsel together about Cuchulain, for their women and their maidens loved him greatly, and it is what they settled among themselves, that they would seek out a young girl that would be a fitting wife for him, the way that their own wives and their daughters would not be making so much of him. And beside that they were afraid he might die young, and leave no heir after him.

So Conchubar sent out nine men into each of the provinces of Ireland to look for a wife for Cuchulain, to see if in any dun or in any chief place, they could find the daughter of a king or of an owner of land or a householder, who would be pleasing to him, that he might ask her in marriage.

All the messengers came back at the end of a year, but not one of them had found a young girl that would please Cuchulain. And then he himself went out to court a young girl he knew in Luglochta Loga, the Garden of Lugh, Emer, the daughter of Forgall Manach, the Wily.

He set out in his chariot, that all the chariots of Ulster could not follow by reason of its swiftness, and of the chariot chief who sat in it. And he found the young girl on her playing field, with her companions about her, daughters of the landowners that lived near Forgall's dun, and they learning needlework and fine embroidery from Emer. And of all the young girls of Ireland, she was the one Cuchulain thought worth courting; for she had the six gifts—the gift of beauty, the gift of voice, the gift of sweet speech, the gift of needlework, the gift of wisdom, the gift of chastity. And Cuchulain had said that no woman should marry him but one that was his equal in age, in appearance, and in race, in kill and handiness; and one who was the best worker with her needle of the young girls of Ireland, for that would be the only one would be a fitting wife for him. And that is why it was Emer he went to ask above all others.

And it was in his rich clothes he went out that day, his crimson five-folded tunic, and his brooch of inlaid gold, and his hooded white shirt, that was embroidered with red gold. And as the young girls were sitting together on their bench on the lawn, they heard coming towards them the clatter of hoofs, the creaking of a chariot, the cracking of straps, the grating of wheels, the rushing of horses, the clanking of arms. "Let one of you see," said Emer, "what is it that is coming towards us." And Fiall, daughter of Forgall, went out and met him, and he came with her to the place where Emer and her companions were, and he wished a blessing to them. Then Emer lifted up her lovely face and saw Cuchulain, and she said, "May the gods make smooth the path before you." "And you," he said "may you be safe from every harm." "Where are you come from?" she asked him. And he answered her in riddles, that her companions might not understand him, and he said, "From Intide Emna." "Where did you sleep?" "We slept," he said, "in the house of the man that tends the cattle of the plain of Tethra." "What was your food there?" "The ruin of a chariot was cooked for us," he said. "Which way did you come?" "Between the two mountains of the wood." "Which way did you take after that?" "That is not hard to tell," he said. "From the Cover of the Sea, over the Great Dam, between the God and his Druid; over the Marrow of the Woman, between the Boar and his Dam; over the Washing-place of the horses of Dea; between the King of Ana and his servant, to Mandchuile of the Four Corners of the World; over Great Crime and the Remnants of the Great Feast; between the Vat and the little Vat, to the Gardens of Lugh, to the daughters of Tethra, the nephew of the King of the Formor." "And what account have you to give of yourself?" said Emer. "I am the nephew of the man that disappears in another in the wood of Badb," said Cuchulain.

"And now, maiden," he said, "what account have you to give of yourself?" "That is not hard to tell," said Emer, "for what should a maiden be but Teamhair upon the hills, a watcher that sees no one, an eel hiding in the water, a rush out of reach. The daughter of a king should be a flame of hospitality, a road that cannot be entered. And I have champions that follow me," she said, "to keep me from whoever would bring me away against their will, and against the will and the knowledge of Forgall, the dark king."

"Who are the champions that follow you, maiden?" said Cuchulain.

"It is not hard to tell you that," said Emer. "Two of the name of Lui; two Luaths, Luath and Lath Goible, sons of Tethra; Triath and Trescath; Brion and Bolor; Bas, son of Omnach; the right Condla, and Cond, son of Forgall. Every man of them has the strength of a hundred and the feats of nine. And it would be hard for me," she said, "to tell of all the many powers Forgall has himself. He is stronger than any labouring man, more learned than any Druid, more quick of mind than any poet. You will have more than your games to do when you fight against Forgall, for many have told of his power and of the strength of his doings."

"Why do you not count me as a strong man as good as those others?" said Cuchulain. "Why would I not indeed, if your doings had been spoken of like theirs?" she said. "I swear by the oath of my people," said Cuchulain, "I will make my doings be spoken of among the great doings of heroes in their strength." "What is your strength, then?" said Emer. "That is easily told: when my strength in fighting is weakest I defend twenty; a third part of my strength is enough for thirty; in my full strength I fight alone against forty; and a hundred are safe under my protection. For dread of me, fighting men avoid fords and battles; armies and armed men go backward from the fear of my face."

"That is a good account for a young boy," said Emer, "but you have not reached yet to the strength of chariot chiefs." "But, indeed," said Cuchulain, "it is well I have been reared by Conchubar, my dear foster-father. It is not as a countryman strives to bring up his children, between the flags and the kneading trough, between the fire and the wall, on the floor of the one room, that Conchubar has brought me up: but is among chariot chiefs and heroes, among jesters and Druids, among poets and learned men, among landowners and farmers of Ulster I have been reared, so that I have all their manners and their gifts."

"Who are these men, then, that have brought you up to do the things you are boasting of?" said Emer.

"That is easily told," he said. "Fair-speaking Sencha taught me wisdom and right judgment; Blai, lord of lands, my kinsman, took me to his house, so that I have entertained the men of Conchubar's province; Fergus brought me up to fights and to battles, so that I am able to use my strength. I stood by the knee of Amergin the poet, he was my tutor, so that I can stand up to any man, I can make praises for the doings of a king. Finchoem helped to rear me, so that Conall Cearnach is my foster-brother. Cathbad of the Gentle Face taught me, for the sake of Dechtire, so that I understand the arts of the Druids, and I have learned all the goodness of knowledge. All the men of Ulster have had a hand in bringing me up, chariot-drivers and chiefs of chariots, kings and chef poets, so that I am the darling of the whole army, so that I fight for the honour of all alike. And as to yourself, Emer," he said, "what way have you been reared in the Garden of Lugh?"

"It is easy to tell you that," said Emer. "I was brought up," she said, "in ancient virtues, in lawful behaviour, in the keeping of chastity, in stateliness of form, in the rank of a queen, in all noble ways among the women of Ireland." "These are good virtues indeed," said Cuchulain. "And why, then, would it not be right for us two to become one? For up to this time," he said, "I have never found a young girl able to hold talk with me the way you have done." "Have you no wife already?" said Emer. "I have not, indeed." "I may not marry before my sister is married," she said then, "for she is older than myself." "Truly it is not with your sister, but with yourself, I have fallen in love," said Cuchulain.

While they were talking like this, Cuchulain saw the breasts of the maiden over the bosom of her dress, and he said: "Fair is this plain, the plain of the noble yoke." And Emer said, "No one comes to this plain who does not overcome as many as a hundred on each ford, from the ford at Ailbine to Banchuig Arcait."

"Fair is the plain, the plain of the noble yoke," said Cuchulain. "No one comes to this plain," said she, "who does not go out in safety from Samhain to Oilmell, and from Oilmell

to Beltaine, and again from Beltaine to Bron Trogain."

"Everything you have commanded, so it will be done by me," said Cuchulain.

"And the offer you have made me, it is accepted, it is taken, it is granted," said Emer.

With that Cuchulain left the place, and they talked no more with one another on that day.

The War
for the Bull of Cuailgne
Lady Gregory

It happened one time before Maeve and Ailell rose up from their royal bed in Cruachan, they began to talk with one another. "It is what I am thinking," said Ailell, "it is a true saying, 'Good is the wife of a good man.'" "A true saying, indeed," said Maeve, "but why do you bring it to mind at this time?" "I bring it to mind now because you are better to-day than the day I married you." "I was good before I ever had to do with you," said Maeve. "How well we never heard of that and never knew it until now," said Ailell, "but only that you stopped at home like any other woman, while the enemies at your boundaries were slaughtering and destroying and driving all before them, and you not able to hinder them." "That is not the way it was at all," said Maeve, "but of the six daughters of my father Eochaid, King of Ireland, I was the best and the one that was thought most of. As to dividing gifts and giving counsel, I was the best of them, and as to battle feats and arms and fighting, I was the best of them. It was I had fifteen hundred soldiers sons of exiles, and fifteen hundred sons of chief men. And I had these," she said, "for my own household; and along with that my father gave me one of the provinces of Ireland, the province of Cruachan; so that Maeve of Cruachan is the name that was given to me."

"And as to being asked in marriage," she said, "messengers came to me from your own brother, Finn, son of Ross Ruadh, king of Leinster, and I gave him a refusal; and after that there came messengers from Cairbre Niafer, son of Rossa, king of Teamhair; and from Conchubar, son of Ness, king of Ulster; and after that again from Eochu Beag, son of Luchta, and I refused them all. For it is not a common marriage portion would have satisfied me, the same as is asked by the other women of Ireland," she said; "but it is what I asked as a marriage portion, a man without stinginess, without jealousy, without fear. For it would not be fitting for me to be with a man that would be close-handed, for my own hand is open in wage-paying and in free-giving; and it would be a reproach on my husband, I to be a better wage-payer than himself. And it would not be fitting for me to be with a man that would be cowardly, for I myself go into struggles and fights and battles and gain the victory; and it would be a reproach to my husband, his wife to be braver than himself. And it would not be fitting for me to be with a husband that would be jealous, for I was never without one man being with me in the shadow of another. Now I have got such a husband as I looked for in yourself, Ailell, for you are not close-handed or jealous or cowardly. And I gave you good wedding gifts," she said, "suits of clothing enough for twelve men; a chariot that was worth three times seven serving-maids; the width of your face in red gold, the round of your arm in a bracelet of white bronze. And the fine or the tribute you can ask of your enemies is no more than the fine or the tribute. I have a right to ask, for you are nothing of yourself, but it is in the pay of a woman you are," she said. "That is not so," said Ailell, "for I am a king's son, and I have two brothers that are kings, Finn, king of Leinster, and Cairbre, king of Teamhair, and I would have been king in their places but that they are older than myself. And as to giving of wages and dividing of gifts," he said, "you are no better than myself; and if this province is under the rule of a woman it is the only province in Ireland that is so; and it is not through your right I took the kingship of it, but through the right of my mother, Mata of Murrisk, daughter of Magach. And if I took the daughter of the chief king of

Ireland for my wife, it was because I thought she was a fitting wife for me." "You know well," said Maeve, "the riches that belong to me are greater than the riches that belong to you." "That is a wonder to me," said Ailell, "for there is no one in Ireland has a better store of jewels and riches and treasure than myself, and you know well there is not."

"Let our goods and our riches be put beside one another, and let a value be put on them," said Maeve, "and you will know which of us owns most." "I am content to do that," said Ailell.

With that, orders were given to their people to bring out their goods and to count them, and to put a value on them. They did so, and the first things they brought out were their drinking vessels, their vats, their iron vessels, and all the things belonging to their households, and they were found to be equal. Then their rings were brought out, and their bracelets and chains and brooches, their clothing of crimson and blue and black and green and yellow and saffron and speckled silks, and these were found to be equal. Then their great flocks of sheep were driven from the green plains of the open country and were counted, and they were found to be equal; and if there was a ram among Maeve's flocks that was the equal of a serving-maid in value, Ailell had one that was as good. And their horses were brought in from the meadows, and their herds of swine out of the woods and the valleys, and they were equal one to another. And the last thing that was done was to bring in the herds of cattle from the forest and the wild places of the province, and when they were put beside one another they were found to be equal, but for one thing only. It happened a bull had been calved in Maeve's herd, and his name was Fionnbanach, the White-horned. But he would not stop in Maeve's herds, for he did not think it fitting to be under the rule of a woman, and he had gone into Ailell's herds and stopped there; and now he was the best bull in the whole province of Connaught. And when Maeve saw him, and knew he was better than any bull in her own, there was great vexation on her, and it was as bad to her as if she did not own one head of cattle at all. So she called Mac Roth, the herald, to her, and bade him to find out where there was a bull as good as the White-horned to be got in any province of the provinces of Ireland.

"I myself know that well," said Mac Roth, "for there is a bull that is twice as good as himself at the house of Daire, son of Fachtna, in the district of Cuailgne." "Rise up, then," said Maeve, "and make no delay, but go to Daire from me, and ask the loan of that bull for a year, and I will return him at the end of the year, and fifty heifers along with him, as fee for the loan. And there is another thing for you to say, Mac Roth; if the people of Daire's district and country think bad of him for sending away that wonderful jewel the Donn of Cuailgne, let Daire himself come along with him, and I will give him the equal of his own lands on the smooth plain of Ai, and a chariot that is worth three times seven serving-maids, and my own close friendship along with that."

So Mac Roth set out on his journey, and nine men along with him, and when they came to Daire's house there was a good welcome before them, as there should be, for Mac Roth was the chief herald of all Ireland.

Daire asked him then what was the reason of his journey, and Mac Roth told him the whole story of the quarrel between Maeve and Ailell and of the counting of their herds, and of the great rewards Maeve offered him if he would give her the loan for one year of the Brown Bull of Cuailgne. Daire was so well pleased when he heard this, that he wagged himself till the stitches of the feathers under him burst, and he said: "I will send him to Maeve into Connaught, whether the men of Ulster like it or do not like it." Mac Roth was well content with that; and he and his men were attended to, and fresh rushes were spread, and a feast was put before them, with every sort of food and of drink, so that after a while they were not so clear in their wits as they were before.

Two of them began talking to one another then, and one said: "This is a good man in whose house we are." "He is good indeed," said the other. "Is there any man in Ulster better than himself?" said the first. "There is, surely," said the other, "for Conchubar the High King is a better man, and it is no shame for all the men of Ulster to gather to him." "It is a wonder," said the first, "Daire to have given up to us what it would have taken the strength of the four provinces of Ireland to bring away by force." "That I may see the mouth that spoke those words filled with blood," said another of the men; "for if Daire had refused to give it willingly, the strength of Ailell and of Maeve, and the knowledge of Fergus, son of Rogh, would have brought it from him against his will."

Just as they were talking, the chief steward of Daire's house came in, and servants along with him bringing meat and drink; and he heard what the men of Connaught said and great anger came on him, and he bade the servants put down the food for them, but he never told them to use it or not to use it, but he went to where Daire was and said: "Was it you, Daire, promised the Brown Bull of Cuailgne to these messengers?" "It was myself indeed," said Daire. "Then what they have said is true?" "What is that?" said Daire. "They say that you knew that if you did not give him willingly you would have had to give him against your will by the strength of Ailell and Maeve and by the guidance of Fergus, son of Rogh." "If they say that," said Daire, "I swear by the gods my people swear by, that they will not take him away till they take him by force."

On the morning of the morrow the messengers rose up and went into the house where Daire was. "Show us now," they said, "the place where the bull is." "I will not indeed," said

Daire; "but if it was a habit with me," he said, "to do treachery to messengers or to travellers or to men on their road, not one of you would go back alive to Cruachan." "What reason have you for this change?" said Mac Roth. "I have a good reason for it, for you were saying last night that if I did not give the bull willingly, I would be forced to give it against my will by Ailell and Maeve and by Fergus." "If that was said, it was the talk of common messengers, and they after eating and drinking," said Mac Roth, "and it is not fitting for you to take notice of a thing like that."

"It may be so" said Daire; "but for all that," he said, "I will not give the bull this time."

They went back then to Cruachan, and Maeve asked news of them, and Mac Roth told her the whole story, how Daire gave them the promise of the bull at first, and refused it afterwards. "What was the reason of that?" she asked. And when it was told her she said: "This riddle is not hard to guess; they did not intend to let us get the bull at all; but now we will take him from them by force," she said.

And this was the cause of the great war for the Brown Bull of Cuailgne.

Concerning Cows
Lady Wilde

The most singular legends of Ireland relate to bulls and cows, and there are hundreds of places all commencing with the word *Bo* (one of the most ancient words in the Irish language), which recall some mystic or mythical story of a cow, especially of a white heifer, which animal seems to have been an object of the greatest veneration from all antiquity.

In old times there arose one day a maiden from the sea, a beautiful Berooch, or mermaid, and all the people on the Western Coast of Erin gathered round her and wondered at her beauty. And the great chief of the land carried her home to his house, where she was treated like a queen.

And she was very gentle and wise, and after some time she acquired the language, and could talk to the people quite well in their own Irish tongue, to their great delight and wonder. Then she informed them that she had been sent to their country by a great spirit, to announce the arrival in Ireland of the three sacred cows—*Bo-Finn, Bo-Ruadh*, and *Bo-Dhu*—the white, the red, and the black cows, who were destined to fill the land with the most splendid cattle, so that the people should never know want while the world lasted.

This was such good news that the people in their delight carried the sea-maiden from house to house in procession, in order that she might tell it herself to every one; and they crowned her with flowers, while the musicians went before her, singing to their harps.

After dwelling with them a little longer she asked to be taken back to the sea, for she had grown sad at being away so long from her own kindred. So, on May Eve, a great crowd accompanied her down to the strand, where she took leave of them, telling them that on that day year they should all assemble at the same place to await the arrival of the three cows. Then she plunged into the sea and was seen no more.

However, on that day year all the people of Ireland assembled on the shore to watch, as they had been directed by the beautiful sea-maiden; and all the high cliffs and all the rocks were covered with anxious spectators from the early dawn. Nor did they wait in vain. Exactly at noon the waves were stirred with a mighty commotion, and three cows rose up from the sea—a white, a red, and a black—all beautiful to behold, with sleek skins, large soft eyes, and curved horns, white as ivory. They stood upon the shore for a while, looking around them. Then each one went in a different direction, by three roads; the black went south, the red went north, and the milk-white heifer—the *Bo-Finn*—crossed the plain of Ireland to the very centre, where stood the king's palace. And every place she passed was named after her, and every well she drank at was called *Lough-na-Bo*, or *Tober-Bo-Fin* (the well of the white cow), so her memory remains to this day.

In process of time the white heifer gave birth to twins, a male and female calf, and from them descended a great race, still existing in Ireland; after which the white cow disappeared into a great cave by the sea, the entrance to which no man knows. And there she remains, and will remain, in an enchanted sleep, until the true king of Eire, the lord of Ireland, shall come to waken her; but the lake near the cave is still known as *Lough-na-Bo-banna* (the lake of the snow-white cow). Yet some say it was the king's daughter was carried off by enchantment to the cave, in the form of a cow, and she will never regain her form until she sleeps on the summit of each of the three highest mountains in Ireland; but only the true king of Eire can wake her from her sleep, and bring her to "the rock of the high place," when she will be restored at last to her own beautiful form.

Another legend says that a red-haired woman struck

the beautiful Bo-Finn with her staff, and smote her to death; and the roar which the white cow gave in dying was heard throughout the whole of Ireland, and all the people trembled. This is evidently an allegory. The beautiful Bo-Finn—the white cow—is Ireland herself; and the red-haired woman who smote her to death was Queen Elizabeth, "in whose time, after her cruel wars, the cry of the slaughtered people was heard all over the land, and went up to heaven for vengeance against the enemies of Ireland; and the kingdom was shaken as by an earthquake, by the roar of the oppressed against the tyrant." The path of the white cow across Ireland is marked by small rude stone monuments, still existing. They show the exact spot where she rested each night and had her bed, and then the adjoining lands have names connected with the tradition— as, "The plain of the Fenian cows;" "The hill of worship;" "The pool of the spotted ox," called after him because he always wanted to drink till the white cows came, for they were much attached to each other.

There are also Druid stones at one resting-place, with Ogham marks on them. Some time ago an endeavour was made to remove and carry off the stones of one of the monuments: but the man who first put a spade in the ground was "struck," and remained bedridden for years.

The plain of the death of the *Bo-Banna* (the white cow), where she gave the roar that shook all Ireland is called "the plain of lamentation." It never was tilled, and never will be tilled. The people hold it as a sacred spot, and until recently it was the custom to have dances there every Sunday. But these old usages are rapidly dying out; for though meant originally as mystic ceremonies, yet by degrees they degenerated to such licentious revelry that the wrath of the priesthood fell on them, and they were discontinued.

There is a holy well near "the plain of lamentation," called *Tobar-na-Bo* (the well of the white cow); and these ancient names, coming down the stream of time from the far-off Pagan era, attest the great antiquity of the legend of the coming to Ireland of the mystic and beautiful *Bo-Finn*.

There is another legend concerning the arrival of the three cows—the white, the red, and the black—which is said to be taken from the Book of Enoch.

Four cows sprang at once from the earth—two white, a red, and a black—and one of the four went over to the white cow and taught it a mystery. And it trembled and became a man, and this was the first man that appeared in Erin. And the man fashioned a ship and dwelt there with the cows while a deluge covered the earth. And when the waters ceased, the red and the black cows went their way, but the white remained.

The story is supposed by Bryant to be a literal rendering of some ancient hieroglyph, descriptive of the three races of mankind, and of the dispersion of the primal human family.

Edain the Queen

Lady Wilde

Now it happened that the king of Munster one day saw a beautiful girl bathing, and he loved her and made her his queen. And in all the land was no woman so lovely to look upon as the fair Edain, and the fame of her beauty came to the ears of the great and powerful chief and king of the Tuatha-de-Danann, Midar by name. So he disguised himself and went to the court of the king of Munster, as a wandering bard, that he might look on the beauty of Edain. And he challenged the king to a game of chess.

"Who is this man that I should play chess with him?" said the king.

"Try me," said the stranger; "you will find me a worthy foe."

Then the king said—"But the chess-board is in the

queen's apartment, and I cannot disturb her."

However, when the queen heard that a stranger had challenged the king to chess, she sent her page in with the chess-board, and then came herself to greet the stranger. And Midar was so dazzled with her beauty, that he could not speak, he could only gaze on her. And the queen also seemed troubled, and after a time she left them alone.

"Now, what shall we play for?" asked the king.

"Let the conqueror name the reward," answered the stranger, "and whatever he desires let it be granted to him."

"Agreed," replied the monarch.

Then they played the game and the stranger won.

"What is your demand now?" cried the king. "I have given my word that whatever you name shall be yours."

"I demand the Lady Edain, the queen, as my reward," replied the stranger. "But I shall not ask you to give her up to me till this day year." And the stranger departed.

Now the king was utterly perplexed and confounded, but he took good note of the time, and on that night just a twelvemonth after, he made a great feast at Tara for all the Princes, and he placed three lines of his chosen warriors all round the palace, and forbade any stranger to enter on pain of death. So all being secure, as he thought, he took his place at the feast with the beautiful Edain beside him, all glittering with jewels and a golden crown on her head, and the revelry went on till midnight. Just then, to his horror, the king looked up, and there stood the stranger in the middle of the hall, but no one seemed to perceive him save only the king. He fixed his eyes on the queen, and coming towards her, he struck the golden harp he had in his hand and sang in a low sweet voice—

> "O Edain, wilt thou come with me
> To a wonderful palace that is mine?
> White are the teeth there, and black the brows,
> And crimson as the mead are the lips of the
> lovers.

> "O, woman, if thou comest to my proud people,
> 'Tis a golden crown shall circle thy head,
> Thou shalt dwell by the sweet streams of my
> land,
> And drink of the mead and wine in the arms of
> thy lover."

Then he gently put his arm around the queen's waist, and drew her up from her royal throne, and went forth with her through the midst of all the guests, none hindering, and the king himself was like one in a dream, and could neither speak nor move. But when he recovered himself, then he knew that the stranger was one of the fairy chiefs of the Tuatha-de-

Danann who had carried off the beautiful Edain to his fairy mansion. So he sent round messengers to all the kings of Erin that they should destroy all the forts of the hated Tuatha race, and slay and kill and let none live till the queen, his young bride, was brought back to him. Still she came not. Then the king out of revenge ordered his men to block up all the stables where the royal horses of the Dananns were kept, so that they might die of hunger; but the horses were of noble blood, and no bars or bolts could hold them, and they broke through all the bars and rushed out like the whirlwind, and spread all over the country. And the kings, when they saw the beauty of the horses, forgot all about the search for Queen Edain, and only strove how they could seize and hold as their own some of the fiery steeds with the silver hoofs and golden bridles. Then the king raged in his wrath, and sent for the chief of the Druids, and told him he should be put to death unless he discovered the place where the queen lay hid. So the Druid went over all Ireland, and searched, and made spells with oghams, and at last, having carved four oghams on four wands of a hazel-tree, it was revealed to him that deep down in a hill in the very centre of Ireland, Queen Edain was hidden away in the enchanted palace of Midar the fairy chief.

Then the king gathered a great army, and they circled the hill, and dug down and down till they came to the very centre; and just as they reached the gate of the fairy palace,

Midar by his enchantments sent forth fifty beautiful women from the hillside, to distract the attention of the warriors, all so like the queen in form and features and dress, that the king himself could not make out truly, if his own wife was amongst them or not. But Edain, when she saw her husband so near her, was touched by love of him in her heart, and the power of the enchantment fell from her soul, and she came to him, and he lifted her up on his horse and kissed her tenderly, and brought her back safely to his royal palace of Tara, where they lived happily ever after.

A Legend of Knockmany
William Carleton

What Irish man, woman, or child has not heard of our renowned Hibernian Hercules, the great and glorious Fin M'Coul? Not one, from Cape Clear to the Giant's Causeway, nor from that back again to Cape Clear. And, by-the-way, speaking of the Giant's Causeway brings me at once to the beginning of my story. Well, it so happened that Fin and his gigantic relatives were all working at the Causeway, in order to make a bridge, or what was still better, a good stout pad-road, across to Scotland; when Fin, who was very fond of his wife Oonagh, took it into his head that he would go home and see how the poor woman got on in his absence. To be sure, Fin was a true Irishman, and so the sorrow thing in life brought him back, only to see that she was snug and comfortable, and, above all things, that she got her rest well at night; for he knew that the poor woman, when he was with her, used to be subject to nightly qualms and configurations, that kept him very anxious, decent man, striving to keep her up to the good spirits and health that she had when they were first married. So, accordingly, he pulled up a fir-tree, and, after lopping off the roots and branches, made a walking stick of it, and set out on his way to Oonagh. Oonagh, or rather Fin, lived at this time on the very tip-top of Knockmany Hill, which faces a cousin of its own called Cullamore, that rises up, half-hill, half-mountain on the opposite side—east-east by south, as the sailors say, when they wish to puzzle a landsman.

Now, the truth is, for it must come out, that honest Fin's attention for his wife, though cordial enough in itself, was by no manner of means the real cause of his journey home. There was at that time another giant, named Cucullin— some say he was Irish, some say he was Scotch—but whether Scotch or Irish, sorrow doubt of it but he was a *targer*. No other giant of the day could stand before him; and such was his strength, that, when well vexed, he could give a stamp that shook the country about him. The fame and name of him went far and near; and nothing in the shape of a man, it was said, had any chance with him in a fight. Whether the story is true or not, I cannot say, but the report went that, by one blow of his fists he flattened a thunderbolt, and kept it in his pocket, in the shape of a pancake, to show all his enemies, when they were about to fight him. Undoubtedly he had given every giant in Ireland a considerable beating, barring Fin M'Coul himself; and he swore, by the solemn contents of Moll Kelly's Primer, that he would never rest, night or day, winter or summer, till he would serve Fin with the same sauce, if he could catch him. Fin, however, who no doubt was the cock of the walk on his own dunghill, had a strong disinclination to meet a giant who could make a young earthquake, or flatten a thunderbolt when he was angry; so he accordingly kept dodging about from place to place, not much to his credit as a Trojan, to be sure, whenever he happened to get the word that Cucullin was on the scent of him. This, then, was the marrow of the whole movement, although he put it on his anxiety to see Oonagh; and I am not saying but there was some truth in that too. However, the short and the long of it was, with reverence be it spoken, that he heard Cucullin was coming to the Causeway to have a trial of strength with him; and he was naturally enough seized, in consequence, with a very warm and sudden sit of affection for his wife, poor woman, who was delicate in her health, and leading, besides, a very lonely uncomfortable life of it (he assured them) in his absence. He accordingly pulled up the fir-tree, as I said before, and having snedded it into a walking stick, set out on his affectionate travels to see

his darling Oonagh on the top of Knockmany, by the way.

In truth, to state the suspicions of the country at the time, the people wondered very much why it was that Fin selected such a windy spot for his dwelling-house, and they even went so far as to tell him as much.

"What can you mane, Mr. M'Coul," said they, "by pitching your tent upon the top of Knockmany, where you never are without a breeze, day or night, winter or summer, and where you're often forced to take your nightcap* without either going to bed or turning up your little finger; ay, an' where, besides this, there's the sorrow's own want of water?"

"Why," said Fin, "ever since I was the height of a round tower, I was known to be fond of having a good prospect of my own; and where the dickens, neighbors, could I find a better spot for a prospect than the top of Knockmany? As for water, I am sinking a pump**, and, plase goodness, as soon as the Causeway's made, I intend to finish it."

Now, this was more of Fin's philosophy; for the real state of the case was, that he pitched upon the top of

---

*A common name for the cloud or rack that hangs, as a forerunner of wet weather, about the peak of a mountain.

**There is upon the top of this hill an opening that bears a very strong resemblance to the crater of an extinct volcano.

Knockmany in order that he might be able to see Cucullin coming towards the house, and, of course, that he himself might go to look after his distant transactions in other parts of the country, rather than—but no matter—we do not wish to be too hard on Fin. All we have to say is, that if he wanted a spot from which to keep a sharp look-out—and, between ourselves, he did want it grievously—barring Slieve Croob, or Slieve Donard, or its own cousin, Cullamore, he could not find a nearer or more convenient situation for it in the sweet and sagacious province of Ulster.

"God save all here!" said Fin, good-humouredly, on putting his honest face into his own door.

"Musha, Fin, avick, an' you're welcome home to your own Oonagh, you darlin' bully." Here followed a smack that is said to have made the waters of the lake at the bottom of the hill curl, as it were, with kindness and sympathy.

"Faith," said Fin, "beautiful; an' how are you, Oonagh—and how did you sport your figure during my absence, my bil-berry?"

"Never a merrier—as bouncing a grass widow as ever there was in sweet 'Tyrone among the bushes'."

Fin gave a short, good-humoured cough, and laughed most heartily, to show her how much he was delighted that she made herself happy in his absence.

"An' what brought you home so soon, Fin?" said she.

"Why, avourneen," said Fin, putting in his answer in the proper way, "never the thing but the purest of love and affection for yourself. Sure you know that's truth, anyhow, Oonagh."

Fin spent two or three happy days with Oonagh, and felt himself very comfortable, considering the dread he had of Cucullin. This, however, grew upon him so much that his wife could not but perceive something lay on his mind which he kept altogether to himself. Let a woman alone, in the meantime, for ferreting or wheedling a secret out of her good man, when she wishes. Fin was a proof of this.

"It's this Cucullin," said he, "that's troubling me. When the fellow gets angry, and begins to stamp, he'll shake you a whole townland; and its well known that he can stop a thunderbolt, for he always carries one about him in the shape of a pancake, to show to anyone that might misdoubt it."

As he spoke, he clapped his thumb in his mouth, which he always did when he wanted to prophecy, or to know anything that happened in his absence; and the wife, who knew what he did it for, said very sweetly,

"Fin, darling, I hope you don't bite your thumb at me, dear?"

"No," said Fin; "but I bite my thumb, acushla," said he.

"Yes, jewel; but take care and don't draw blood," said she. "Ah, Fin! don't, my bully—don't."

"He's coming," said Fin; "I see him below Dungannon."

"Thank goodness, dear! an' who is it, avick? Glory be to God!"

"That baste, Cucullin," replied Fin; "and how to manage I don't know. If I run away, I am disgraced; and I know that sooner or later I must meet him, for my thumb tells me so."

"When will he be here?" said she.

"Tomorrow, about two o'clock," replied Fin, with a groan.

"Well, my bully, don't be cast down," said Oonagh; "depend on me, and maybe I'll bring you better out of this scrape than ever you could bring yourself, by your rule o' thumb."

This quieted Fin's heart very much, for he knew that Oonagh was hand and glove with the fairies; and, indeed, to tell the truth, she was supposed to be a fairy herself. If she was, however, she must have been a kind-hearted one, for, by all accounts, she never did anything but good in the neighourhood.

Now it so happened that Oonagh had a sister named Granua, living opposite them, on the very top of Cullamore, which I have mentioned already, and this Granua was quite as powerful as herself. The beautiful valley that lies between them is not more than about three or four miles broad, so that of a summer's evening, Granua and Oonagh were able to hold many an agreeable conversation across it, from the one hilltop to the other. Upon this occasion Oonagh resolved to consult her sister as to what was best to be done in the difficulty that surrounded them.

"Granua," said she, "are you at home?"

"No," said the other; "I'm picking bilberries in Althadhawan" (Anglicé, the Devil's Glen).

"Well," said Oonagh, "get up to the top of Cullamore, look about you, and then tell us what you see."

"Very well," replied Granua; after a few minutes, "I am there now."

"What do you see?" asked the other.

"Goodness be about us!" exclaimed Granua, "I see the biggest giant that ever was known coming up from Dungannon."

"Ay," said Oonagh, "there's our difficulty. That giant is the great Cucullin; and he's now commin' up to leather Fin. What's to be done?"

"I'll call to him," she replied, "to come up to Cullamore and refresh himself, and maybe that will give you and Fin time to think of some plan to get yourselves out of the scrape. But," she proceeded, "I'm short of butter, having in the house only half-a-dozen firkins, and as I'm to have a few giants and giantesses to spend the evening with me, I'd feel thankful, Oonagh, if you'd throw me up fifteen or sixteen tubs, or the largest miscaun you have got, and you'll oblige me very much."

"I'll do that with a heart and a-half," replied Oonagh; "and, indeed, Granua, I feel myself under great obligations to you for your kindness in keeping him off us till we see what can be done; for what would become of us all if anything happened to Fin, poor man."

She accordingly got the largest miscaun of butter she had—which might be about the size of a couple a dozen mill-stones, so that you might easily judge of its size—and calling up to her sister, "Granua," said she,"are you ready? I'm going to throw you up a miscaun, so be prepared to catch it."

"I will," said the other; "a good throw now, and take care it does not fall short."

Oonagh threw it; but, in consequence of her anxiety about Fin and Cucullin, she forgot to say the charm that was to send it up, so that, instead of reaching Cullamore, as she expected, it fell about half-way between the two hills, at the edge of the Broad Bog near Augher.

"My curse upon you!" she exclaimed; "you've disgraced me. I now change you into a grey stone. Lie there as a testimony of what has happened; and may evil betide the first living man that will ever attempt to remove or injure you!"

And, sure enough, there it lies to this day, with the mark of the four fingers and thumb imprinted in it, exactly as it came out of her hand.

"Never mind," said Granua, "I must only do the best I

can with Cucullin. If all fail, I'll give him a cast of heather broth to keep the wind out of his stomach, or a panada of oak-bark to draw it in a bit; but, above all things, think of some plan to get Fin out of the scrape he's in, otherwise he's a lost man. You know you used to be sharp and ready-witted; and my own opinion, Oonagh, is, that it will go hard with you, or you'll outdo Cucullin yet."

She then made a high smoke on the top of the hill, after which she put her finger in her mouth, and gave three whistles, and by that Cucullin knew he was invited to Cullamore—for this was the way that the Irish long ago gave a sign to all strangers and travellers, to let them know they were welcome to come and take share of whatever was going.

In the meantime, Fin was very melancholy, and did not know what to do, or how to act at all. Cucullin was an ugly customer, no doubt, to meet with; and, moreover, the idea of the confounded "cake" aforesaid flattened the very heart within him. What chance could he have, strong and brave though he was, with a man who could, when put in a passion, walk the country into earthquakes and knock thunderbolts into pancakes? The thing was impossible; and Fin knew not on what hand to turn him. Right or left— backward or forward—where to go he could form no guess whatsoever.

"Oonagh," he said, "can you do nothing for me? Where's all your intervention? Am I to be skivered like a rabbit before your eyes, and to have my name disgraced forever in the sight of all my tribe, and me the best man among them? How am I to fight this man-mountain—this huge cross between an earthquake and a thunderbolt? —with a pancake in his pocket that was once——"

"Be easy, Fin," replied Oonagh; "troth, I'm ashamed of you. Keep your toe in your pump, will you? Talking of pancakes, maybe we'll give him as good as any he brings with him—thunderbolt or otherwise. If I don't treat him to as smart feeding as he's got this many a day, never trust Oonagh again. Leave him to me, and do just as I bid you."

This relieved Fin very much; for, after all, he had great confidence in his wife, knowing, as he did, that she had got him out of many a quandry before. The present, however, was the greatest of all; but still he began to get courage, and was able to eat his victuals as usual. Oonagh then drew the nine woollen threads of different colours, which she always did to find out the best way of succeeding in anything of importance she went about. She then platted them into three platts with three colours in each, putting one on her right arm, one round her heart, and the third round her right ankle, for then she knew that nothing could fail with her that she undertook.

Having everything now prepared, she sent round to the neighbours and borrowed one-and-twenty iron griddles, which she took and kneaded into the hearts of one-and-

The Hill of Tara, Co. Meath. (Photo: QT Pictures.) Once the symbolic seat of the High Kings of Ireland. According to legend it was here, at Tara (Irish: "Teamhair") that the mythical heroes gathered, seated according to their status. Storytellers and poets had places of honor beside the king. Much of the action of early Irish tales takes place in this venerated spot.

Sunrise Over Lough Gill, Co. Sligo. (Photo: Peter Zoeller.) One of the mythic, mysterious lakes of Ireland, complete with a solitary swan, reminds one of the sorrowful legend of *The Children of Lir* in which the four children of King Lir are changed into white swans by their jealous stepmother.

White Rocks, Co. Antrim. (Photo: Christopher Hill.) A dramatic display of imposing rocks create mythical intrigue to the shoreline of Northern Ireland. There is never a want of material to stimulate imagination and fantasy in the Irish land- or seascape. Mystery, magic, and a sense of the Otherworld—a realm beyond the senses—abounds.

Giant's Causeway, Co. Antrim. (Photo: Liam Blake.) History tells us that this collection of tubular basalt structures is the result of volcanic action millions of years ago, but according to legend the giant Finn McCool built the promontory as a pathway across the sea to Scotland.

Gortnavern Dolmen, Co. Donegal. (Photo: Liam Blake.) Dolmen are stunning, sculptural, megalithic tombs. This one in the romantic landscape of Donegal has been marked "Grania's Bed" on old maps, referring to the flight of Diarmuid and Grania from the furious, deceived, aged Finn McCool.

Old Farm Cottage, The Mourne Mountains, Co. Down. (Photo: George Munday.)
The impressive scenic backdrop of the Mourne mountains adds majesty and
plenty of granite to the quintessential Irish countryside with its green fields,
stone farm structures, and endless stone walls.

twenty cakes of bread, and these she baked on the fire in the usual way, setting them aside in the cupboard according as they were done. She then put down a large pot of new milk, which she made into curds and whey, and gave Fin due instructions how to use the curds when Cucullin should come. Having done all this, she sat down quite contented, waiting for his arrival on the next day about two o'clock, that being the hour at which he was expected—for Fin knew as much by the sucking of his thumb. Now, this was a curious property that Fin's thumb had; but notwithstanding all the wisdom and logic he used, to suck out of it, it could never have stood to him here were it not for the wit of his wife. In this very thing, moreover, he was very much resembled by his great foe, Cucullin; for it was well known that the huge strength he possessed all lay in the middle finger of his right hand, and that, if he happened by any mischance to lose it, he was no more, notwithstanding his bulk, than a common man.

At length, the next day, he was seen coming across the valley, and Oonagh knew that it was time to commence operations. She immediately made the cradle, and desired Fin to lay down in it, and cover himself up with the clothes.

"You must pass for your own child," said she; "so just lie there snug, and say nothing, but be guided by me." This, to be sure, was wormwood to Fin—I mean going into the cradle in such a cowardly manner—but he knew Oonagh well; and finding that he had nothing else for it, with a very rueful face he gathered himself into it, and lay snug, as she had desired him.

About two o'clock, as he had been expected, Cucullin came in. "God save all here!" said he; "is this where the great Fin M'Coul lives?"

"Indeed it is, honest man," replied Oonagh; "God save you kindly—won't you be sitting?"

"Thank you, ma'am," says he, sitting down; "you're Mrs. M'Coul, I suppose?"

"I am," said she; "and I have no reason, I hope, to be ashamed of my husband."

"No," said the other, "he has the name of being the strongest and bravest man in Ireland; but for all that, there's a man not far from you that's very desirous of taking a shake with him. Is he at home?"

"Why, then, no," she replied; "and if ever a man left his house in a fury, he did. It appears that some one told him of a big basthoon of a giant called Cucullin being down at the Causeway to look for him, and so he set out there to try if he could catch him. Troth, I hope, for the poor giant's sake, he won't meet with him, for if he does, Fin will make paste of him at once."

"Well," said the other, "I am Cuchullin, and I have been seeking him these twelve months, but he always kept clear of me; and I will never rest night or day till I lay my hands on him."

At this Oonagh set up a loud laugh, of great contempt, by-the-way, and looked at him as if he was only a mere handful of a man.

"Did you ever see Fin?" said she, changing her manner all at once.

"How could I?" said he; "he always took care to keep his distance."

"I thought so," she replied; "I judged as much; and if you take my advice, you poor-looking creature, you'll pray night and day that you may never see him, for I tell you it will be a black day for you when you do. But, in the meantime, you perceive that the wind's on the door, and as Fin himself is from home, maybe you'd be civil enough to turn the house, for it's always what Fin does when he's here."

This was a startler even to Cuchullin; but he got up, however, and after pulling the middle finger of his right hand until it cracked three times, he went outside, and getting his arms about the house, completely turned it as she had wished. When Fin saw this, he felt a certain description of moisture, which shall be nameless, oozing out through every pore of his skin; but Oonagh, depending upon her woman's wit, felt not a whit daunted.

"Arrah, then," said she, "as you are so civil, maybe you'd do another obliging turn for us, as Fin's not here to do it himself. You see, after this long stretch of dry weather we've had, we feel very badly off for want of water. Now, Fin says there's a fine spring well somewhere under the rocks behind the hill here below, and it was his intention to pull them asunder; but having heard of you, he left the place in such a fury, that he never thought of it. Now, if you try to find it, troth I'd feel it a kindness."

She then brought Cucullin down to see the place, which was then all one solid rock; and after looking at it for some time, he cracked his right middle finger nine times, and, stooping down, tore a cleft about four hundred feet deep, and a quarter of a mile in length, which has since been christened by the name of Lumford's Glen. This feat nearly threw Oonagh herself off her guard; but what won't a woman's sagacity and presence of mind accomplish?

"You'll come in now," said she, "and eat a bit of such humble fare as we can give you. Fin, even although he and you are enemies, would scorn not to treat you kindly in his own house; and, indeed, if I didn't do it even in his absence, he would not be pleased with me."

She accordingly brought him in, and placing half-a-dozen of the cakes we spoke of before him, together with a can or two of butter, a side of boiled bacon, and a stack of cabbage, she desired him to help himself—for this, be it known, was long before the invention of potatoes. Cuchullin, who, by the way, was a glutton as well as a hero, put one of the cakes in his mouth to take a huge whack out of it, when both Fin and Oonagh were stunned with a noise that resembled something between a growl and a yell. "Blood and fury!" he shouted; "how is this? Here are two of my teeth out! What kind of bread is this you gave me?"

"What's the matter?" said Oonagh coolly.

"Matter!" shouted the other again; "why, here are the two best teeth in my head gone."

"Why," said she, "that's Fin's bread—the only bread he ever eats when at home; but, indeed, I forgot to tell you that nobody can eat it but himself, and that child in the cradle there. I thought, however, that as you were reported to be rather a stout little fellow of your size, you might be able to manage it, and I did not wish to affront a man that thinks himself able to fight Fin. Here's another cake—maybe it's not so hard as that."

Cuchullin at the moment was not only hungry, but ravenous, so he accordingly made a fresh set at the second cake, and immediately another yell was heard twice as loud as the first. "Thunder and giblets!" he roared, "take your bread out of this, or I will not have a tooth in my head; there's another pair of them gone!"

"Well, honest man," replied Oonagh, "if you're not able to eat the bread, say so quietly, and don't be wakening the child in the cradle there. There, now, he's awake upon me."

Fin now gave a skirl that startled the giant, as coming from such a youngster as he was represented to be. "Mother," said he, "I'm hungry—get me something to eat." Oonagh went over, and putting into his hand a cake that had no griddle in it, Fin, whose appetite in the meantime was sharpened by what he saw going forward, soon made it disappear. Cuchullin was thunderstruck, and secretly thanked his stars that he had the good fortune to miss meeting Fin, for, as he said to himself, I'd have no chance with a man who could eat such bread as that, which even his son that's but in his cradle can munch before my eyes.

"I'd like to take a glimpse at the lad in the cradle," said he to Oonagh; "for I can tell you that the infant who can manage that nutriment is no joke to look at, or to feed of a scarce summer."

"With all the veins of my heart," replied Oonagh "get up, acushla, and show this decent little man something that won't be unworthy of your father, Fin M'Coul."

Fin, who was dressed for the occasion as much like a boy as possible, got up, and bringing Cuchullin out, "Are you strong?" said he.

"Thunder an' ounds!" exclaimed the other, "what a voice in so small a chap!"

"Are you strong?" said Fin again; "are you able to squeeze water out of that white stone?" he asked, putting one into Cuchullin's hand. The latter squeezed and squeezed the stone, but to no purpose; he might pull the rocks of Lumford's Glen asunder, and flatten a thunderbolt, but to squeeze water out of a white stone was beyond his strength. Fin eyed him with great contempt, as he kept straining and squeezing and squeezing and straining, till he got black in the face with the efforts.

"Ah, you're a poor creature!" said Fin. "You, a giant! Give me the stone here, and when I'll show you what Fin's little son can do; you may then judge of what my daddy himself is."

Fin then took the stone, and slyly exchanging it for the curds, he squeezed the latter until the whey, as clear as water, oozed out in a little shower from his hand.

"I'll now go in," said he "to my cradle; for I scorn to lose my time with any one that's not able to eat my daddy's bread or squeeze water out of a stone. Bedad, you had better be off out of this before he comes back; for if he catches you, it's in flummery he'd have you in two minutes."

Cucullin, seeing what he had seen, was of the same opinion himself; his knees knocked together with the terror of Fin's return, and he accordingly hastened in to bid Oonagh farewell, and to assure her, that from that day out, he never wished to hear of, much less to see, her husband. "I admit fairly that I'm not a match for him," said he, "strong as I am;

tell him I will avoid him as I would the plague, and that I will make myself scarce in this part of the country while I live."

Fin, in the meantime, had gone into the cradle, where he lay very quietly, his heart at his mouth with delight that Cucullin was about to take his departure, without discovering the tricks that had been played off on him.

"It's well for you," said Oonagh, "that he doesn't happen to be here, for it's nothing but hawk's meat he'd make of you."

"I know that," says Cucullin; "divil a thing else he'd make of me; but before I go, will you let me feel what kind of teeth they are that can eat griddle-bread like that?"—and he pointed to it as he spoke.

"With all pleasure in life," said she; "only, as they're far back in his head, you must put your finger a good way in."

Cucullin was surprised to find such a powerful set of grinders in one so young; but he was still much more so on finding, when he took his hand from Fin's mouth, that he had left the very finger upon which his whole strength depended, behind him. He gave one loud groan, and fell down at once with terror and weakness. This was all Fin wanted, who now knew that his most powerful and bitterest enemy was completely at his mercy. He instantly started out of the cradle, and in a few minutes the great Cucullin, that was for such a length of time the terror of him and all his followers, lay a corpse before him. Thus did Fin, through the wit and invention of Oonagh, his wife, succeed in overcoming his enemy by stratagem, which he never could have done by force: and thus also is it proved that the women, if they bring us into many an unpleasant scrap, can sometimes succeed in getting us out of others that are as bad.

The Giant's Stairs

Thomas Crofton Croker

On the road between Passage
and Cork there is an old mansion called Ronayne's Court. It
may be easily known from the stack of chimneys and the
gable-ends, which are to be seen, look at it which way you
will. Here it was that Maurice Ronayne and his wife Margaret
Gould kept house, as may be learned to this day from the great
old chimney-piece, on which is carved their arms. They were a
mighty worthy couple, and had but one son, who was called
Philip, after no less a person than the King of Spain.

Immediately on his smelling the cold air of this world
the child sneezed, which was naturally taken to be a good sign

of his having a clear head; and the subsequent rapidity of his learning was truly amazing, for on the very first day a primer was put into his hands he tore out the A, B, C page and destroyed it, as a thing quite beneath his notice. No wonder, then, that both father and mother were proud of their heir, who gave such indisputable proofs of genius, or, as they called it in that part of the world, *"genus."*

One morning, however, Master Phil, who was then just seven years old, was missing, and no one could tell what had become of him: servants were sent in all directions to seek him, on horseback and on foot, but they returned without any tidings of the boy, whose disappearance altogether was most unaccountable. A large reward was offered, but it produced them no intelligence, and years rolled away without Mr. and Mrs. Ronayne having obtained any satisfactory account of the fate of their lost child.

There lived at this time, near Carigaline, one Robert Kelly, a blacksmith by trade. He was what is termed a handy man, and his abilities were held in much estimation by the lads and lasses of the neighbourhood; for, independent of shoeing horses, which he did to great perfection, and making plough-irons, he interpreted dreams for the young women, sung "Arthur O'Bradley" at their weddings, and was so good-natured a fellow at a christening, that he was gossip to half the country round.

Now it happened that Robin had a dream himself, and young Philip Ronayne appeared to him in it, at the dead hour of the night. Robin thought he saw the boy mounted upon a beautiful white horse, and that he told him how he was made a page to the giant Mahon MacMahon, who had carried him off, and who held his court in the hard heart of the rock. "The seven years—my time of service—are clean out, Robin," said he, "and if you release me this night I will be the making of you for ever after."

"And how will I know," said Robin—cunning enough, even in his sleep— "but this is all a dream?"

"Take that," said the boy, "for a token"—and at the word the white horse struck out with one of his hind legs, and gave poor Robin such a kick in the forehead that, thinking he was a dead man, he roared as loud as he could after his brains, and woke up, calling a thousand murders. He found himself in bed, but he had the mark of the blow, the regular print of a horse-shoe, upon his forehead as red as blood; and Robin Kelly, who never before found himself puzzled at the dream of any other person, did not know what to think of his own.

Robin was well acquainted with the Giant's Stairs as, indeed, who is not that knows the harbour? They consist of great masses of rock, which, piled one above another, rise like a flight of steps from the very deep water, against the bold cliff of Carrigmahon. Nor are they badly suited for stairs to those who have legs of sufficient length to stride over a moderate-sized house, or to enable them to clear the space of a mile in a hop, step, and jump. Both these feats the giant MacMahon was said to have performed in the days of Finnian glory; and the common tradition of the country placed his dwelling within the cliff up whose side the stairs led.

Such was the impression which the dream made on Robin, that he determined to put its truth to the test. It occurred to him, however, before setting out on this adventure, that a plough-iron may be no bad companion, as, from experience, he knew it was an excellent knock-down argument, having on more occasions than one settled a little disagreement very quietly; so, putting one on his shoulder, off he marched, in the cool of the evening, through Glaun a Thowk (the Hawk's Glen) to Monkstown. Here an old gossip of his (Tom Clancey by name) lived, who, on hearing Robin's dream, promised him the use of his skiff, and, moreover, offered to assist in rowing it to the Giant's Stairs.

After a supper, which was of the best, they embarked. It was a beautiful still night, and the little boat glided swiftly along. The regular dip of the oars, the distant song of the sailor, and sometimes the voice of a belated traveller at the ferry of Carrigaloe, alone broke the quietness of the land and sea and sky. The tide was in their favour, and in a few minutes Robin and his gossip rested on their oars under the dark shadow of the Giant's Stairs. Robin looked anxiously for the entrance to the Giant's Palace, which, it was said, may be found by any one seeking it at midnight; but no such entrance could he see. His impatience had hurried him there before that time, and after waiting a considerable space in a state of suspense not to be described, Robin, with pure vexation, could not help exclaiming to his companion, " 'Tis a pair of fools we are, Tom Clancey, for coming here at all on the strength of a dream."

"And whose doing is it," said Tom, "but your own?"

At the moment he spoke they perceived a faint glimmering of light to proceed from the cliff, which gradually increased until a porch big enough for a king's palace unfolded itself almost on a level with the water. They pulled the skiff directly towards the opening, and Robin Kelly, seizing his plough-iron, boldly entered with a strong hand and a stout heart. Wild and strange was that entrance, the whole of which appeared formed of grim and grotesque faces, blending so strangely each with the other that it was impossible to define any: the chin of one formed the nose of another; what appeared to be a fixed and stern eye, if dwelt upon, changed to a gaping mouth; and the lines of the lofty forehead grew into a majestic and flowing beard. The more Robin allowed himself to contemplate the forms around him, the more terrific they became; and the stoney expression of this crowd of faces assumed a savage ferocity as his imagination converted feature after feature into a different shape and character. Losing the twilight in which these indefinite forms were visible, he advanced through a dark and devious passage, whilst a deep and rumbling noise sounded as if the rock was about to close upon him, and swallow him up alive for ever. Now, indeed, poor Robin felt afraid.

"Robin, Robin," said he, "if you were a fool for coming here, what in the name of fortune are you now?" But, as before, he had scarcely spoken, when he saw a small light twinkling through the darkness of the distance, like a star in the midnight sky. To retreat was out of the question; for so many turnings and windings were in the passage, that he considered he had but little chance of making his way back. He, therefore, proceeded towards the bit of light, and came at last into a spacious chamber, from the roof of which hung the solitary lamp that had guided him. Emerging from such profound gloom, the single lamp afforded Robin abundant light to discover several gigantic figures seated round a massive stone table, as if in serious deliberation, but no word disturbed the breathless silence which prevailed. At the head of this table sat Mahon MacMahon himself, whose majestic beard had taken root, and in the course of ages grown into a stone slab. He was the first who perceived Robin; and instantly starting up, drew his long beard from the huge piece of rock in such haste and with so sudden a jerk that it was shattered into a thousand pieces.

"What seek you?" he demanded in a voice of thunder.

"I come," answered Robin, with as much boldness as he could put on, for his heart was almost fainting within him; "I come," said he, "to claim Philip Ronayne, whose time of service is out this night."

"And who sent you here?" said the giant.

"'Twas of my own accord I came," said Robin.

"Then you must single him out from among my pages," said the giant; "and if you fix on the wrong one, your life is the forfeit. Follow me." He led Robin into a hall of vast extent, and filled with lights; along either side of which were rows of beautiful children, all apparently seven years old, and none beyond that age, dressed in green, and every one exactly dressed alike.

"Here," said Mahon, "you are free to take Philip Ronayne, if you will; but, remember, I give but one choice."

Robin was sadly perplexed; for there were hundreds upon hundreds of children; and he had no very clear recollection of the boy he sought. But he walked along the hall, by the side of Mahon, as if nothing was the matter, although his great iron dress clanked fearfully at every step, sounding louder than Robin's own sledge battering on his anvil.

They had nearly reached the end without speaking, when Robin, seeing that the only means he had was to make friends with the giant, determined to try what effect a few soft words might have on him.

" 'Tis a fine wholesome appearance the poor children carry," remarked Robin, "although they have been here so long shut out from the fresh air and the blessed light of heaven. 'Tis tenderly your honour must have reared them!"

"Aye," said the giant, "that is true for you; so give me your hand; for you are, I believe, a very honest fellow for a blacksmith."

Robin at the first look did not much like the huge size of the hand, and, therefore, presented his plough-iron, which the giant seizing, twisted in his grasp round and round again as if it had been a potato stalk. On seeing this all the children set up a shout of laughter. In the midst of their mirth Robin thought he heard his name called; and all ear and eye, he put his hand on the boy who he fancied had spoken, crying out at the same time, "Let me live or die for it, but this is young Phil Ronayne."

"It is Philip Ronayne—happy Philip Ronayne," said his young companions; and in an instant the hall became dark. Crashing noises were heard, and all was in strange confusion; but Robin held fast his prize, and found himself lying in the grey dawn of the morning at the head of the Giant's Stairs with the boy clasped in his arms.

Robin had plenty of gossips to spread the story of his wonderful adventure: Passage, Monkstown, Carigaline—the whole barony of Kerricurrihy rung with it.

"Are you quite sure, Robin, it is young Phil Ronayne you have brought back with you?" was the regular question; for although the boy had been seven years away, his appearance now was just the same as on the day he was missed. He had neither grown taller nor older in look, and he spoke of things which had happened before he was carried off as one awakened from sleep, or as if they had occurred yesterday.

"Am I sure?" Well, that's a queer question," was Robin's reply; "seeing the boy has the blue eye of the mother, with the foxy hair of the father; to say nothing of the purty wart on the right side of his little nose."

However Robin Kelly may have been questioned, the worthy couple of Ronayne's Court doubted not that he was the deliverer of their child from the power of the Giant

MacMahon; and the reward they bestowed on him equalled their gratitude.

Philip Ronayne lived to be an old man; and he was remarkable to the day of his death for his skill in working brass and iron, which it was believed he had learned during his seven years' apprenticeship to the Giant Mahon MacMahon.

Lough Neagh

Lady Augusta Wilde

Wonderful tales are related about the formation of Lough Neagh; and the whole country round abounds with traditions. One of them affirms that the great Fionn Ma-Coul, being in a rage one day, took up a handful of earth and flung it into the sea; and the handful as of such a size that where it fell it formed the Isle of Man, and the hollow caused by its removal became the basin of the present Lough Neagh.

Another legend is that a holy well once existed in the locality, blessed and sanctified by a saint with wonderful miraculous powers of healing; provided that every patient on leaving, after cure, carefully closed the wicket-gate that shut in the well. But once, however, a woman having forgotten this information, left the gate open, when instantly the indignant waters sprang from their bed and pursued the offender, who fled in terror before the advancing waves, until at last she sank down exhausted, when the waters closed over her, and she was no more seen. But along the track of her flight the waters remained, and formed the great lake now existing, which is exactly the length the woman traversed in her flight from the angry spirit of the lake.

Mysterious influences still haunt the locality all round Lough Neagh; for it is the most ancient dwelling-place of the fairies, and when they pass at night from one island to another, soft music is heard floating by, and then the boatmen know that fairies are out for a pleasure trip; and one man even averred that he saw them going by in the track of the moon-beam, a crowd of little men all dressed in green with red caps, and the ladies in silver gossamer. And he liked these pretty creatures, and always left a little poteen for them in the bottle when he was on the island. In return for which attention they gave him the best of good luck in fishing and in everything else; for never a gauger came next or nigh his place while the fairies protected him, and many a time they led the gauger into a bog, and otherwise discomfited him, when he and his men were after a still.

So the fisherman loved his little friends, and they took great care of him; for even in the troublous times of '98, when the wreckers were all over the country, they did him no harm;

though indeed the same wreckers knew where to find a good glass of something when they came his way, and he always gave it to them with a heart and a half; for didn't they tell him they were going to free Ireland from the Sassenach tyranny.

Down deep, under the waters of Lough Neagh, can still be seen, by those who have the gift of fairy vision, the columns and walls of the beautiful palaces once inhabited by the fairy race when they were the gods of the earth; and this tradition of a buried town beneath the waves has been prevalent for centuries amongst the people.

Giraldus Cambrensis states, that in his time the tops of towers, "built after the fashion of the country," were distinctly visible in calm, clear weather, under the surface of the lake; and still the fairies haunt the ruins of their former splendour, and hold festivals beneath the waters when the full moon is shining; for the boatmen, coming home late at night, have often heard sweet music rising up from beneath the waves and the sound of laughter, and seen glimmering lights far down under the water, where the ancient fairy palaces are supposed to be.

The Legend of O'Donoghue

Thomas Crofton Croker

In an age so distant that the precise period is unknown, a chieftain named O'Donoghue ruled over the country which surrounds the romantic Lough Lean, now called the Lake of Killarney. Wisdom, beneficence and justice distinguished his reign, and the prosperity and happiness of his subjects were their natural results. He is said to have been as renowned for his warlike exploits as for his pacific virtues; and as a proof that his domestic administration was not the less rigorous because it was mild, a rocky island is pointed out to strangers, called "O'Donoghue's Prison," in which this prince once confined his own son for some act of disorder and disobedience.

His end—for it cannot correctly be called his death— was singular and mysterious. At one of those splendid feasts for which his court was celebrated, surrounded by the most distinguished of his subjects, he was engaged in a prophetic relation of the events which were to happen in ages yet to come. His auditors listened, now wrapt in wonder, now fired with indignation, burning with shame, or melted into sorrow, as he faithfully detailed the heroism, the injuries, the crimes and the miseries of their descendants. In the midst of his predictions, he rose slowly from his seat, advanced with a solemn, measured, and majestic tread to the shore of the lake, and walked forward composedly upon its unyielding surface. When he had nearly reached the centre, he paused for a moment, then turning slowly round, looked towards his friends, and waving his arms to them with the cheerful air of one taking a short farewell, disappeared from their view.

The memory of the good O'Donoghue has been cherished by successive generations with affectionate reverence: and it is believed that at sunrise, on every May-dew morning—the anniversary of his departure—he revisits his ancient domains. A favoured few only are in general permitted to see him, and this distinction is always an omen of good fortune to the beholders: when it is granted to many, it is a sure token of an abundant harvest—a blessing, the want of which during this prince's reign was never felt by his people.

Some years have elapsed since the last appearance of O'Donoghue. The April of that year had been remarkably wild and stormy; but on May morning the fury of the elements had altogether subsided. The air was hushed and still; and the sky, which was reflected in the serene lake, resembled a beautiful but deceitful countenance, whose smiles, after the most tempestuous emotions, tempt the stranger to believe that it belongs to a soul which no passion has ever ruffled.

The first beams of the rising sun were just gliding the lofty summit of Glenaa, when the waters near the eastern shores of the lake became suddenly and violently agitated, though all the rest of its surface lay smooth and still as a tomb of polished marble; the next moment a foaming wave darted forward, and, like a proud, high-crested war-horse, exulting in his strength, rushed across the lake towards Toomies Mountain. Behind this wave appeared a stately warrior fully armed, mounted upon a milk-white steed; his snowy plume waved gracefully from a helmet of polished steel, and at his back fluttered a light blue scarf. The horse, apparently exulting in his noble burden, sprang after the wave along the water, which bore him up like firm earth, while showers of spray that glittered brightly in the morning sun were dashed up at every bound.

The warrior was O'Donoghue; he was followed by numberless youths and maidens who moved lightly and unconstrained over the watery plain, as the moonlight fairies glide through the fields of air; they were linked together by garlands of delicious spring flowers, and they timed their movements to strains of enchanting melody. When

O'Donoghue had nearly reached the western side of the lake, he suddenly turned his steed, and directed his course along the wood-fringed shore of Glenaa, preceded by the huge wave that curled and foamed up as high as the horse's neck, whose fiery nostrils snorted above it. The long train of attendants followed with playful deviations the track of their leader, and moved on with unabated fleetness to their celestial music, till gradually, as they entered the narrow strait between Glenaa and Dinis, they became involved in the mists which still partially floated over the lakes, and faded from the view of the wondering beholders; but the sound of their music still fell upon the ear, and echo, catching up the harmonious strains, fondly repeated and prolonged them in soft and softer tones, till the last faint repetition died away, and the hearers awoke as from a dream of bliss.

The Enchanted Lake
Thomas Crofton Croker

In the west of Ireland there was a lake, and no doubt it is there still, in which many young men had been at various times drowned. What made the circumstance remarkable was that the bodies of the drowned persons were never found. People naturally wondered at this, and at length the lake came to have a bad repute. Many dreadful stories were told about that lake. Some would affirm that on a dark night its waters appeared like fire; others would speak of horrid forms which were seen to glide over it; and everyone agrees that a strange, sulphureous smell issued from out of it.

There lived not far distant from this lake a young farmer, named Roderick Keating, who was about to be married to one of the prettiest girls in that part of the country. On his return from Limerick, where he had been to purchase the wedding ring, he came up with two or three of his acquaintances, who were standing on the shore, and they began to joke with him about Peggy Honan. One said that young Delaney, his rival, had in his absence contrived to win the affection of his mistress. But Roderick's confidence in his intended bride was too great to be disturbed at this tale; and putting his hand in his pocket, he produced and held up with a significant look the wedding ring. As he was turning it between his fore-finger and thumb, in token of triumph, some-how or other the ring rolled from his hand and fell into the lake. Roderick looked after it with the greatest sorrow; it was not so much for its value, though it had cost him half-a-guinea, as for the ill-luck of the thing; and the water was so deep that there was little chance of recovering it. His compan-ions laughed at him, and he in vain endeavoured to tempt any of them by the offer of a handsome reward to dive after the ring. They were all as little inclined to venture as Roderick Keating himself; for the tales which they had heard when chil-dren were strongly impressed on their memories, and a super-stitious dread filled the mind of each.

"Must I, then, go back to Limerick to buy another ring?" exclaimed the farmer. "Will not ten times what the ring cost tempt anyone of you to venture after it?"

There was within hearing a man who was considered to be a poor, crazy, half-witted fellow, but he was as harmless as a child, and used to go wandering up and down through the country from one place to another. When he heard of so great a reward, Paddeen—for that was his name—spoke out, and said that if Roderick Keating would give him encouragement equal to what he had offered to the others, he was ready to venture after the ring into the lake; and Paddeen, all the while he spoke, looked as covetous after the sport as the money.

"I'll take you at your word," said Keating. So Paddeen pulled off his coat, and without a single syllable more, down he plunged, head foremost, into the lake. What depth he went to, no one can tell exactly; but he was going, going, going down through the water, until the water parted from him, and he came upon the dry land. The sky, and the light, and everything, was there just as it is here; and he saw fine pleasure-grounds, with an elegant avenue through them, and a grand house, with a power of steps going up to the door. When he had recovered from his wonder at finding land so dry and comfortable under the water, he looked about him, and what should he see but all the young men that were drowned working away in the pleasure-grounds as if nothing had ever happened to them! Some of them were mowing down the grass, and more were setting out the gravel walks, and doing all manner of nice work, as neat and as clever as if they had never been drowned; and they were singing away with high glee:

"She is fair as Cappoquin;
Have you courage her to win?
And her wealth it far outshines
Cullen's bog and Silvermines.
She exceeds all heart can wish;
Not brawling like the Foherish,
But as the brightly flowing Lee,
Graceful, mild, and pure is she!"

Well, Paddeen could not but look at the young men, for he knew some of them before they were lost in the lake; but he said nothing, though he thought a great deal more, for all that, like an oyster—no, not the wind of a word passed his lips; so on he went towards the big house, bold enough, as if he had seen nothing to speak of, yet all the time mightily wishing to know who the young woman could be that the young men were singing the song about.

When he had nearly reached the door of the great house, out walks from the kitchen a powerful fat woman, moving along like a beer-barrel on two legs, with teeth as big as horses' teeth, and up she made towards him.

"Good morrow, Paddeen!" said she.

"Good morrow, ma'am!" said he.

"What brought you here?" said she.

" 'Tis after Rory Keating's gold ring," said he, "I'm come."

"Here it is for you," said Paddeen's fat friend, with a smile on her face that moved like boiling stirabout [gruel].

"Thank you, ma'am," replied Paddeen, taking it from her. "I need not say the Lord increase you, for you're fat enough already. Will you tell me, if you please, am I to go back the same way I came?"

"Then you did not come to marry me?" cried the corpulent woman, in a desperate fury.

"Just wait till I come back again, my darling," said Paddeen. "I'm to be paid for my message, and I must return with the answer, or else they'll wonder what has become of me."

"Never mind the money," said the fat woman. "If you marry me, you shall live for ever and a day in that house, and want for nothing."

Paddeen saw clearly that, having got possession of the ring, the fat woman had no power to detain him; so without minding anything she said, he kept moving and moving down the avenue, quite quietly, and looking about him; for, to tell the truth, he had no particular inclination to marry a fat fairy.

When he came to the gate, without ever saying good-bye, out he bolted, and he found the water coming all about him again. Up he plunged through it, and wonder enough there was when Paddeen was seen swimming away at the opposite side of the lake; but he soon made the shore, and told Roderick Keating and the other boys that were standing there looking out for him all that had happened. Roderick paid him the five guineas for the ring on the spot; and Paddeen thought himself so rich with such a sum of money in his pocket that he did not go back to marry the fat lady with the fine house at the bottom of the lake, knowing she had plenty of young men to choose a husband from, if she pleased to be married.

Fior Usga
Thomas Crofton Croker

A little way beyond the Gallows Green of Cork and just outside the town, there is a great lough of water, where people in the winter go and skate for the sake of diversion; but the sport above the water is nothing to what is under it, for at the very bottom of this lough there are buildings and gardens far more beautiful than any now to be seen; and how they came there was in this manner:

Long before Saxon foot pressed Irish ground there was a great king called Corc, whose palace stood where the lough now is, in a round green valley, that was just a mile about. In the middle of the courtyard was a spring of fair water, so pure and so clear that it was the wonder of all the world. Much did the king rejoice at having so great a curiosity within his palace; but as people came in crowds from far and near to draw the precious water of this spring, he was sorely afraid that in time it might become dry; so he caused a high wall to be built up round it, and would allow nobody to have the water, which was a very great loss to the poor people living about the palace. Whenever he wanted any for himself, he would send his daughter to get it, not liking to trust his servants with the key of the well-door, fearing that they might give some away.

One night the King gave a grand entertainment, and there were many great princes present, and lords and nobles without end; and there were wonderful doings throughout the palace: there were bonfires, whose blaze reached up to the very sky; and dancing was there, to such sweet music that it ought to have waked up the dead out of their graves; and feasting was there in the greatest of plenty for all who came; nor was anyone turned away from the palace gates, but "You're welcome—you're welcome heartily," was the porter's salute for all.

Now, it happened at this grand entertainment there was one young prince above all the rest mighty comely to behold, and as tall and as straight as ever eye would wish to look on. Right merrily did he dance that night with the old king's daughter, wheeling here and wheeling there, as light as a feather, and footing it away to the admiration of every-one. The musicians played the better for seeing their dancing;

and they danced as if their lives depended on it. After all this dancing came the supper, and the young prince was seated at table by the side of his beautiful partner, who smiled upon him as often as he spoke to her; and that was by no means so often as he wishes, for he had constantly to turn to the company and thank them for the many compliments passed upon his fair partner and himself.

In the midst of the banquet, one of the great lords said to King Corc: "May it please your Majesty, here is everything in abundance that heart can wish for, both to eat and drink, except for water."

"Water!" said the King, mightily pleased at someone calling for that of which purposefully there was a want. "Water shall you have, my lord, speedily, and that of such a delicious kind, that I challenge all the world to equal it. Daughter," said he, "go fetch some in the golden vessel which I caused to be made for the purpose."

The King's daughter, who was called Fior Usga (which signifies, in English, Spring Water), did not much like to be told to perform so menial a service before so many people, and though she did not venture to refuse the commands of her father, yet hesitated to obey him, and looked down upon the ground. The King, who loved his daughter very much, seeing this, was sorry for what he desired her to do, but having said the word, he was never known to recall it; he therefore thought of a way to make his daughter go speedily and fetch the water, and it was by proposing that the young prince her partner should go along with her. Accordingly, with a loud voice, he said: "Daughter, I wonder not at your fearing to go alone so late at night; but I doubt not the young prince at your side will go with you." The prince was not displeased at hearing this; and taking the golden vessel in one hand, with the other led the king's daughter out of the hall so gracefully that all present gazed after them with delight.

When they came to the spring of water in the courtyard of the palace, the fair Usga unlocked the door with the greatest care, and stooping down with the golden vessel to take some of the water out of the well, found the vessel so heavy that she lost her balance and fell in. The young prince tried in vain to save her, for the water rose and rose so fast that the entire courtyard was speedily covered with it, and hastened back almost in a state of distraction to the King.

The door of the well being left open, the water, which had been so long confined, rejoiced at obtaining its liberty, rushed forth incessantly, every moment rising higher and higher, and was in the hall of the entertainment sooner than the young prince himself, so that when he attempted to speak to the king he was up to his neck in water. At length the water rose to such a height that it filled the whole of the green valley

in which the king's palace stood, and so the present lough of Cork was formed.

Yet the King and his guests were not drowned, as would now happen if such an awful inundation were to take place; neither was his daughter, the fair Usga, who returned to the banquet-hall the very next night after this dreadful event; and every night since the same entertainment and dancing goes on in the palace at the bottom of the lough, and will last until someone has the luck to bring up out of it the golden vessel which was the cause of all this mischief.

Nobody can doubt that it was a judgment upon the King for his shutting up the well in the courtyard from the poor people; and if there are any who do not credit my story, they may go and see the lough of Cork, for there it is to be seen to this day; the road to Kinsale passes at one side of it; and when its waters are low and clear, the tops of towers and stately buildings may be plainly viewed in the bottom by those who have good eyesight, without the help of spectacles.

The Brown Bear
of Norway
Patrick Kennedy

There was once a king in Ireland, and he had three daughters, and very nice princesses they were. And one day that their father and themselves were walking in the lawn, the king began to joke on them, and to ask them who they would like to be married to. "I'll have the King of Ulster for a husband," says one; "and I'll have the King of Munster," says another; "and," says the youngest, "I'll have no husband but the Brown Bear of Norway." For a nurse of her used to be telling her of an enchanted prince that she called by that name, and she fell in love with him, and his name was the first name on her lips, for the very night before she was dreaming of him. Well, one laughed, and another laughed and they joked on the princess all the rest of the evening. But that very night she woke up out of her sleep in a great hall that was lighted with a thousand lamps; the richest carpets were on the floor, and the walls were covered with cloth of gold and silver, and the place was full of grand company, and the very beautiful prince she saw in her dreams was there, and it wasn't a moment till he was on his knees before her, and telling how much he loved, and asking her wouldn't she be his queen. Well, she hadn't the heart to refuse him, and married they were the same evening.

"Now, my darling," says he, when they were left by themselves, "you must know that I'm under enchantment. A sorceress, that had a beautiful daughter, wished me for her son-in-law; and because I did not keep the young girl at the distance I ought, the mother got power over me, and when I refused to marry her daughter, she made me take the form of a bear by day, and I was to continue so till a lady would marry me of her own free will, and endure five years of great trials after."

Well, when the princess woke in the morning, she missed her husband from her side, and spent the day very sorrowful. But as soon as the lamps were lighted in the grand hall, where she was sitting on a sofa covered with silk, the folding doors flew open and he was sitting by her side the next minute. So they spent another evening so happy, and he took an opportunity of warning her that whenever she began to tire of him, they would be parted forever, and he'd be obliged to marry the witch's daughter.

So she got used to him absent by day, and they spent a happy twelvemonth together, and at last a beautiful little boy was born; and as happy as she was before, she was twice as happy now, for she had her child to keep her company in the day when she couldn't see her husband.

At last, one evening, when herself, and himself and her child, were sitting with a window open because it was a sultry night in flew an eagle, took the infant's sash in his beak, and flew up in the air with him. She screamed and was going to throw herself out through the window after him, but the prince caught her, and looked at her very seriously. She thought of what he said soon after their marriage, and she stopped the cries and complaints that were on her lips. She spent her days very lonely for another twelvemonth, when a beautiful little girl was sent to her. Then she thought to herself she'd have a sharp eye about her this time; so she never would allow a window to be more than a few inches open.

But all her care was in vain. Another evening, when they were all so happy, and the prince dandling the baby, a beautiful greyhound bitch stood before them, took the child out of the father's hand, and was out of the door, before you could wink. This time, she shouted, and ran out of the room, but there was some of the servants in the next room, and all declared that neither child nor dog passed out. She felt, she could not tell how, to her husband, but still she kept command over herself, and didn't once reproach him.

When the third child was born, she would hardly allow a window or a door to be left open for a moment; but she wasn't the nearer to keep the child to herself. They were sitting one evening by the fire, when a lady appeared standing by them. She opened her eyes in a great fright, and stared at her, and while she was doing so, the appearance wrapped a shawl around the baby that was sitting in its father's lap, and either sunk through the ground with it or went up through the wide chimney. This time the mother kept her bed for a month.

"My dear," said she to her husband, when she was beginning to recover, "I think I'd feel better if I was after seeing my father, and mother, and sisters once more. If you give me leave to go home for a few days, I'd be glad." "Very well," said he, "I will do that; and whenever you feel inclined to return, only mention your wish when you lie down at night." The next morning when she awoke, she found herself in her own old chamber in her father's palace. She rung the bell, and in a short time she had her mother, and father, and married sisters about her, and they laughed till they cried for joy at finding her safe back.

So in time she told them all that happened to her, and they didn't know what to advise her to do. She was as fond of her husband as ever, and said she was sure that he couldn't help letting the children go; but still she was afraid beyond the world to have another child to be torn from her. Well, the mother and sisters consulted a wise woman that used to bring eggs to the castle, for they had great confidence in her wisdom. She said the only plan was to secure the bear's skin that the prince was obliged to put on every morning, and get it burned, and then he couldn't help being a man night and day, and then the enchantment would be at an end.

So they all persuaded her to do that, and she promised she would; and after eight days she felt so great a longing to see her husband again, that she made the wish the same night, and when she woke three hours after, she was in her husband's palace, and himself was watching over her. There was great joy on both sides, and they were happy for many days.

Now she began to reflect how she never felt her husband leaving her of a morning, and how she never found him neglecting to give her a sweet drink out of a gold cup just as she was going to bed.

So one night she contrived not to drink any of it, though she pretended to do so; and she was awakeful enough in the morning, and saw her husband passing out through a panel in the wainscot, though she kept her eyelids nearly closed. The next night she got a few drops of the sleepy posset that she saved the evening before, and put it into her huband's night drink, and that made him sleep sound enough. She got up after midnight, passed through the panel, and found a

beautiful brown bear's hide hanging in an alcove. She stole back, and went down to the parlour fire, and put the hide in the middle of it till it was all fine ashes. She then lay down by her husband, gave him a kiss on the cheek, and fell asleep.

If she was to live a hundred years, she'd never forget how she wakened next morning, and found her husband looking down on her with misery and anger in his face. "Unhappy woman," said he, "you have separated us forever! Why hadn't you patience for five years? I am now obliged, whether I like it or not, to go a three days' journey to the witch's castle, and live with her daughter. The skin that was my guard you have burned it, and the egg-wife that gave you the counsel was the witch herself. I won't reproach you; your punishment will be severe enough without it. Farewell for ever!"

He kissed her for the last time, and was off the next minute walking as fast as he could. She shouted after him, and then seeing there was no use, she dressed herself and pursued him. He never stopped, nor stayed, nor looked back, and still she kept him in sight; and when he was on the hill she was in the hollow, and when he was in the hollow she was on the hill. Her life was almost leaving her, when just as the sun was setting, he turned up a bohyeen, and went into a little house. She crawled up after him, and when she got inside there was a beautiful boy on his knees, and he kissing and hugging him. "Here, my poor darling," says he, "is your eldest child, and there," says he, pointing to a nice middle-aged woman that was looking on with a smile on her face, "is the eagle that carried him away." She forgot all her sorrows in a moment, hugging her child, and laughing and crying over him. The Vanithee washed their feet, and rubbed them with an ointment that took all the soreness out of their bones, and made them as fresh as a daisy. Next morning, just before sunrise, he was up and prepared to be off. "Here," he said to her, "is a thing which may be of use to you. It's a scissors, and whatever stuff you cut with it will be turned into rich silk. The moment the sun rises, I'll lose all memory of yourself and the children, but I'll get it at sunset again; farewell." But he wasn't far gone till she was in sight of him again, leaving her boy behind. It was the same to-day as yesterday; their shadows went before them in the morning, and followed them in the evening. He never stopped, and she never stopped, and as the sun was setting, he turned up another lane, and there they found their little daughter. It was all joy and comfort again till morning, and then the third day's journey commenced.

But before he went off, he gave her a comb, and told her that whenever she used it, pearls and diamonds would fall from her hair. Still he had his full memory from sunset to sunrise; but from sunrise to sunset he travelled on under the charm, and never threw his eye behind. This night they came to where the youngest baby was, and the next morning, just before sunrise, the prince spoke to her for the last time. "Here, my poor wife," said he, "is a little hand-reel, with a gold thread that has no end, and the half of our marriage ring. If you can ever get to my bed, put your half ring to mine, I will recollect you. There is a wood yonder, and the moment I enter it, I will forget everything that ever happened between us, as if I was born yesterday. Farewell, dear wife and child, forever." Just then the sun rose, and away he walked towards the wood. She saw it open before him, and close after him, and when she came up, she could no more get in than she could break through a stone wall. She wrung her hands, and shed tears, but then she recollected herself, and cried out, "Wood, I charge you by my three magic gifts—the scissors, the comb, the reel—to let me through;" and it opened, and she went along a walk till she came in sight of a palace, and a lawn, and a woodman's cottage in the edge of the wood where it came nearest the palace.

She went into this lodge, and asked the woodman and his wife to take her into their service. They were not willing at first; but she told them she would ask no wages, and would give them diamonds, and pearls, and silk stuffs, and gold threads whenever they wished for them. So they agreed to let her stay.

It wasn't long till she heard how a young prince, that was just arrived, was living in the palace as the husband of the young mistress. Herself and her mother said that they were married fifteen years before, and that he was charmed away from them ever since. He seldom stirred abroad, and every one that saw him remarked how silent and sorrowful he went about, like a person that was searching for some lost thing.

The servants and folks at the big house began to take notice of the beautiful young woman at the lodge, and to annoy her with their impudent addresses. The head-footman was the most troublesome, and at last she invited him to come take tea with her. Oh, how rejoiced he was, and how he bragged of it in the servants' hall! Well, the evening came, and the footman walked into the lodge and was shown to her sitting-room; for the lodge-keeper and his wife stood in great awe of her, and gave her two nice rooms to herself. Well, he sat down as stiff as a ramrod, and was talking in a grand style about the great doings at the castle, while she was getting the tea and toast ready. "Oh," says she to him, "would you put your hand out at the window, and cut me off a sprig or two of honey-suckle?" He got up in great glee, and put out his hand and head; and said she, "By the virtue of my magic gifts, let a pair of horns spring out of your head, and serenade the lodge." Just as she wishes, so it was. They sprung from the front of each ear, and tore round the walls till they met at the back. Oh the poor wretch! and how he bawled and roared! and the servants that he used to be boasting to, were soon flocking from the castle, and grinning, and huzzaing, and beating tunes on tongs, and shovels, and pans; and he cursing and swearing, and the eyes ready to start out of his head, and he so black in his face, and kicking out his legs behind like mad.

At last she pitied his case, and removed the charm, and the horns dropped down on the ground, and he would have killed her on the spot, only he was weak as water, and his fellow-servants came in, and carried him up to the big house.

Well, some way or other, the story came to the ears of the prince, and he strolled down that way. She had only the dress of a country-woman on her as she sat sewing at the window, but that did not hide her beauty, and he was greatly puzzled and disturbed after he had a good look at her features, just as a body is perplexed to know whether something happened to him when he was young, or if he only dreamed it. Well, the witch's daughter heard about it, too, and she came to see the strange girl; and what did she find her doing, but cutting out the pattern of a gown from brown paper; and as she cut away, the paper became the richest silk she ever saw. The lady looked on with very covetous eyes, and says she, "What would you be satisfied to take for that scissors?" "I'll take nothing," says she, "but leave to spend one night in the prince's chamber, and I'll swear to be as innocent of any crime next morning as we were in the evening." Well, the proud lady fired up, and was going to say something dreadful; but the scissors kept on cutting, and the silk grew richer and richer every inch. So she agreed, and made her take a great oath to keep her promise.

When night came on she was let into her husband's chamber, and the door was locked. But, when she came in a tremble, and sat by the bed-side, the prince was in such a dead sleep, that all she did couldn't wake him. She sung this verse to him, sighing and sobbing, and kept singing it the night long, and it was all in vain:

> "Four long years I was married to thee;
> Three sweet babes I bore to thee;
> Brown Bear of Norway, won't you turn to me?"

At the first dawn, the proud lady was in the chamber, and led her away, and the footman of the horns put out his tongue at her as she was quitting the palace.

So, there was no luck so far; but the next day the prince passed by again, and looked at her and saluted her kindly, as a prince might a farmer's daughter, and passed on; and soon the witch's daughter came by, and found her combing her hair, and pearls and diamonds dropping from it.

Well, another bargain was made, and the princess spent another night of sorrow, and she left the castle at daybreak, and the footman was at his post, and enjoyed his revenge.

The third day the prince went by, and stopped to talk with the strange woman. He asked her could he do anything to serve her, and she said he might. She asked him did he ever wake at night. He said that he was rather wakeful than otherwise; but that during the last two nights, he was listening to a sweet song in his dreams, and could not wake, and that the voice was one that he must have known and loved in some other world long ago. Says she, "Did you drink any sleepy posset either of these evenings before you went to bed?" "I did," said he. "The two evenings my wife gave me something to drink, but I don't know whether it was a sleepy posset or not." "Well, prince," said she, "as you say you would wish to oblige me, you can do it by not tasting any drink this afternoon." "I will not," says he, and then he went on his walk.

Well, the great lady came soon after the prince, and found the stranger using her hand-reel and winding threads of gold off, and the third bargain was made.

That evening the prince was lying on his bed at twilight, and his mind much disturbed; and the door opened, and in his princess walked, and down she sat by his bed-side, and sung:—

"Four long years I was married to thee;
Three sweet babes I bore to thee;
Brown Bear of Norway, won't you turn to me?"

"Brown Bear of Norway!" said he. "I don't understand you." "Don't you remember, prince, that I was your wedded wife for four years?" "I do not," said he, "but I'm sure I wish it was so." "Don't you remember our three babies, that are still alive?" "Show me them. My mind is all a heap of confusion." "Look for the half of our marriage ring, that hangs at your neck, and fit it to this." He did so, and the same moment the charm was broken. His full memory came back on him, and he flung his arms round his wife's neck, and both burst into tears.

Well, there was a great cry outside, and the castle walls were heard splitting and cracking. Every one in the castle was alarmed, and made their way out. The prince and princess went with the rest, and by the time all were safe on the lawn, down came the building, and made the ground tremble for miles round. No one ever saw the witch and her daughter afterwards. It was not long till the prince and princess had their children with them, and then they set out for their own palace. The kings of Ireland, and of Munster and Ulster, and their wives, soon came to visit them, and may every one that deserves it be as happy as the Brown Bear of Norway and his family.

Jack the Master
and Jack the Servant
Patrick Kennedy

There was once a poor couple, and they had three sons, and the youngest's name was Jack. One harvest day, the eldest fellow threw down his hook, and says he, "What's the use to be slaving this way? I'll go seek my fortune;" and the second son said the very same; and says Jack, "I'll go seek my fortune along with you, but let us first leave the harvest stacked for the old couple." Well, he over-persuaded them, and, bedad, as soon as it was safe, they kissed their father and mother, and off they set, every one with three pounds in his pocket, promising to be home in a year and a day. The first night they found no better lodging than a fine dry dyke of a ditch, outside of a churchyard. Before they went to sleep, the youngest got inside to read the tombstone and what should he stumble over but a coffin and the sod was just taken off where the grave was to be. "Some poor body," says he, "that was without friends to put him in consecrated ground: he musn't be left this way." so he threw off his coat, and had a couple of feet cleared out, when a terrible giant walked up. "What are you at?" says he. "The corpse owed me a guinea, and he shan't be buried till it is paid." "Well, here is your guinea," says Jack, "and leave the churchyard, it's nothing the better for your company." Well, he got down a couple of feet more, when another uglier giant again, with two heads on him, came and stopped Jack, with the same story, and got his guinea; and when the grave was six feet down, the third giant looks on him and he had three heads. So Jack was obliged to part with his three guineas before he could put the sod over the poor man. Then he went and lay down by his brothers, and slept till the sun began to shine on their faces next morning.

Well, they soon came to a cross-roads, and there every one took his own way. Jack told them how all his money was gone, but not a farthing did they offer him. After some time, Jack found himself hungry, and so he sat down by the roadside, and pulled out a piece of cake and a lump of bacon. Just as he had the first bit in his mouth, up comes a poor man, and asks something of him, for God's sake. "I have neither brass, gold, nor silver about me," says Jack; "and here's all the provisions I'm master of. Sit down and have a share." Well, the poor man didn't require much pressing, and when the meal was over, says he, "Sir, where are you bound for?" "Faith, I don't know," says Jack; "I'm going to seek my fortune." "I'll go with you for your servant," says the other. "Servant indeed! bad I want a servant—I, that's looking out for a place myself." "No matter. You gave Christian burial to my poor brother yesterday evening. He appeared to me in a dream, and told me where I'd find you, and that I was to be your servant for a year. So you'll be Jack the master, and I Jack the servant." "Well, let it be so."

After sunset, they came to a castle in a wood, and "Here," says the servant, "lives the giant with one head, that wouldn't let my poor brother be buried." He took hold of a club that hung by the door, and gave two or three thravallys on it. "What do you want?" says the giant, looking out through a grating. "Oh, sir, honey!" says Jack, "we want to save you. The king is sending 100,000 men to take your life for all the wickedness you ever done to poor travellers, and that. So because you let my brother be buried, I came to help you." "Oh murdher, murdher, what'll I do at all, at all?" says he. "Have you e'er a hiding-place?" says Jack. "I have a cave, seven miles long, and it opens into the bawn." "That'll do. Leave a good supper for the men, and then don't stir out of your pew till I call you." So they went in, and the giant left a good supper for the army, and went down, and they shut the trap-door down on him.

Well, they ate and they drank, and then Jack got all the horses and cows and drove them over and hether the trap-door, and such fighting and shouting, whinnying and lowing as they had and such a noise as they made! Then Jack opened the door and called out, "Are you there, sir?" "I am," says he, from a mile or two inside. "Wor you frightened, sire?" "You may say frightened. Are they gone away?" "Dickens ago they'll go till you give them your sword of sharpness." "Cock them up with the sword of sharpness. I won't give them a smite of it." "Well, I think you're right. Look out. They'll be down with you in the twinkling of a harrow pin. Go to the end of the cave, and they won't have your head for an hour to come." "Well, that's no great odds; you'll find it in the closet in the parlour. D——do 'em good with it." "Very well," says Jack; "when they're all cleared off, I'll drop a big stone on the trap-door." So the two Jacks slept very comfortable in the giant's bed—it was big enough for the two of them; and next morning, after breakfast, they dropped the big stone on the trap-door, and away they went. That night they slept at the castle of the two-headed giant, and got his cloak of darkness in the same way; and the next night they slept at the castle of the three-headed giant, and got his shoes of swiftness; and the next night they were near the king's palace. "Now," says Jack the servant, "this king has a daughter, and she was so proud that eleven princes killed themselves for her, because she would not marry any of them. At last the King of Morocco thought to persuade her, and the dickens a bit of him she'd have no more nor the others. So he fell on his sword, and died; and the old boy got leave to give him a kind of life again, to punish the proud lady, and he lives in a palace one side of the river, and the king's palace is on the other, and he has got power over the princess and her father; and when they have the heads of twelve courtiers over the gates, the King of Morocco will have the princess to himself and maybe the evil spirit will have them both. Every young man that offers himself has to do three things, and if he fails in all, up goes his head. There you see them—eleven, all black and white, with the sun and rain. You must try your hand. God is stronger than the devil."

So they came to the gate. "What do you want?" says the guard. "I want to marry the princess." "Do you see them heads? Yours will be along with them before you're a week older." "That's my own look out," says Jack. "Well, go on. God help all foolish people!" The king was on his throne in the big hall, and the princess sitting on a golden chair by his side. "Death or my daughter, I suppose," says the king to Jack the master. "Just so, my liege," says Jack. "Very well," says the king. "I don't know whether I'm glad or sorry," says he. "If you don't succeed in three things, my daughter must marry the King of Morocco. If you do succeed, I suppose we'll be eased from the dog's life we are leading. I'll leave my daughter's scissors in your bedroom to-night, and you'll find no going in till morning. If you have the scissors still at sunrise, your head will be safe for that day. Next day you must run a race against the King of Morocco, and if you win, your head will be safe that day, too. Next day, you must bring me the King of Morocco's head, or your own head, then all this bother will be over one way or the other."

Well, they gave the two a good supper, and one time the princess would look sweet at Jack, and another sour; for you know she was under enchantment. Sometimes she'd wish him killed, sometimes she'd wish him to be saved.

When they went into their bedroom, the king came in with them, and laid the scissors on the table. "Mind that," says he, "and I'm sure I don't know whether I wish to find it there tomorrow or not." Well, poor Jack was a little frightened, but his man encouraged him. "Go to bed," says he; "I'll put on the cloak of darkness, and watch, and I hope you'll find the scissors there at sunrise." Well, bedad, he couldn't go to sleep; he kept his eyes on the scissors till the dead hour, and the moment it struck twelve no scissors could he see: it vanished as clean as a whistle. He looked here, there, and everywhere— no scissors. "Well," says he, "there's hope still. Are you there, Jack?" but no answer came. "I can do no more," says he. "I'll go to bed." And to bed he went, and slept.

Just as the clock was striking, Jack in the cloak saw the

wall opening, and the princess walking in, going over to the table, taking up the scissors, and walking out again. He followed her into the garden, and there he saw herself and her twelve maids going down to the boat that was lying by the bank. "I'm in," says the princess. "I'm in," says one maid; and "I'm in," says another; and so on till all were in; "and I'm in," says Jack. "Who's that?" says the last maid. "Go look," says Jack. Well they were all a bit frightened. When they got over, they walked up to the King of Morocco's palace, and there the King of Morocco was to receive them, and give them the best of eating and drinking, and make his musicians play the finest music for them.

When they were coming away, says the princess, "Here's the scissors; mind it or not as you like." "Oh, won't I mind it!" says he. "Here you go," says he again, opening a chest, and dropping it into it, and locking it up with three locks. But before he shut down the lid, Jack in the cloak picked up the scissors, and put it safe into his pocket. Well, when they came to the boat, the same things were said, and the maids were frightened again.

When Jack the master awoke in the morning, the first thing he saw was the scissors on the table, and the next thing he saw was his man lying asleep in the other bed, the next was the cloak of darkness hanging on the bed's foot. Well, he got up, and he danced, and he sung, and he hugged Jack; and when the king came in with a troubled face, there was the scissors safe and sound. "Well, Jack," says he, "you're safe for one more day." And the king and princess were more *meentrach* to Jack to-day than they were yesterday, but the next day the race was to be run.

At last the hour of noon came, and there was the King of Morocco with his hair and his eyes as black as a crow, and his face as yellow as a kite's claw. Jack was there too, and on his feet were the shoes of swiftness. When the bugle blew, they were off, and Jack went seven times round the course while the king went one: it was like the fish in the water, the arrow from a bow, the stone from a sling, or a star shooting in the night. When the race was won, and the people were shouting, the black king looked at Jack like the very devil himself, and, says he: "Don't holloa till you're out of the wood—tomorrow your head or mine." "Heaven is stronger than hell," says Jack.

And now the princess began to wish in earnest that Jack would win, for two parts of the charm were broke. So one of her maids told Jack the servant that she should pay her visit to the Black Fellow at midnight like every other night past. Jack in the cloak was in the garden when the hour came, and they all said the same words, and rowed over, and went up to the palace like they done before.

The King of Morocco was in great fear and anger, and

scolded the princess, but she didn't seem to mind it, and when they were leaving she said, "You know to-morrow is to have your head or Jack's head off. I suppose you will stay up all night!" He was standing on the grass when they were getting into the boat, and just as the last maid had the foot on the edge of it, Jack the servant swept off his head with the sword of sharpness just as if it was the head of a thistle, and put it under his cloak. The body fell on the grass and made no noise. Well, the same moment the princess felt any liking she had for him all gone like last year's snow, and she began to sob and cry for fear of anything happening to Jack. But the maids were not very good at all, and so, from the moment they got out of the boat, Jack kept knocking the head against their legs and their faces, and made them roar and bawl till they were inside the palace.

The first thing Jack the master saw when he woke in the morning, was the black head on the table, and didn't he jump up in a hurry. When the sun was rising, every one in the palace, great and small, were in the bawn before Jack's window, and the king was at the door. "Jack," says he, "if you haven't the King of Morocco's head on a gad, your own will be on a spear, my poor fellow." But just at the moment he heard a great shout from the bawn, and Jack the servant was after opening the window, holding out the King of Morocco's head by the long black hair.

So the princess, and the king, and all were in joy, and maybe they didn't keep the wedding long a-waiting. A year and a day after Jack left home, himself and his wife were in their coach at the cross-roads, and there were the two brothers, sleeping in the ditch with their reaping-hooks by their sides. They wouldn't believe Jack at first that he was their brother, and then they were ready to eat their nails for not sharing with him that day twelve-month. They found their father and mother alive, and you may be sure they left them comfortable. So you see what a good thing in the end it is to be charitable to the poor, dead or alive.

Fin MacCumhail and the Fenians of Erin in the Castle of Fear Dubh

Jeremiah Curtin

It was the custom with Fin MacCumhail and the Fenians of Erin, when a stranger from any part of the world came to their castle, not to ask him a question for a year and a day.

On a time, a champion came to Fin and his men, and remained with them. He was not at all pleasant or agreeable.

At last Fin and his men took counsel together; they were much annoyed because their guest was so dull and morose, never saying a word, always silent.

While discussing what kind of man he was, Diarmuid Duivne offered to try him; so one evening when they were eating together, Diarmuid came and snatched from his mouth the hind-quarter of a bullock, which he was picking.

Diarmuid pulled at one part of the quarter,—pulled with all his strength, but only took the part that he seized, while the other kept the part he held. All laughed; the stranger laughed too, as heartily as any. It was the first laugh they had heard from him.

The strange champion saw all their feats of arms and practised with them, till the year and a day were over. Then he said to Fin and his men:

"I have spent a pleasant year in your company; you gave me good treatment, and the least I can do now is to give you a feast at my own castle."

No one had asked what his name was up to that time. Fin now asked his name. He answered: "My name is Fear Dubh, of Alba."

Fin accepted the invitation: and they appointed the day for the feast, which was to be in Erin, since Fear Dubh did not wish to trouble them to go to Alban. He took leave of his host and started for home.

When the day for the feast came, Fin and the chief men of the Fenians of Erin set out for the castle of Fear Dubh.

They went, a glen at a step, a hill at a leap, and thirty-two miles at a running leap, till they came to the grand castle where the feast was to be given.

They went in; everything was ready, seats at the table,

and every man's name at his seat in the same order as at Fin's castle. Diarmuid, who was always very sportive,—fond of hunting, and paying court to women, was not with them; he had gone to the mountains with his dogs.

All sat down, except Conal Maol MacMorna (never a man spoke well of him); no seat was ready for him, for he used to lie on the flat of his back on the floor, at Fin's castle.

When all were seated the door of the castle closed of itself. Fin then asked the man nearest the door, to rise and open it. The man tried to rise; he pulled this way and that, over and hither, but he couldn't get up. Then the next man tried, and the next, and so on, till the turn came to Fin himself, who tried in vain.

Now, whenever Fin and his men were in trouble and great danger it was their custom to raise a cry of distress (a voice of howling), heard all over Erin. Then all men knew that they were in peril of death; for they never raised this cry except in the last extremity.

Fin's son, Fialan, who was three years old and in the cradle, heard the cry, was roused, and jumped up.

"Get me a sword!" said he to the nurse. "My father and his men are in distress; I must go to aid them."

"What could you do, poor little child?"

Fialan looked around, saw an old rusty sword-blade

laid aside for ages. He took it down, gave it a snap; it sprang up so as to hit his arm, and all the rust dropped off; the blade was pure as shining silver.

"This will do," said he; and then he set out towards the place where he heard the cry, going a glen at a step, a hill at a leap, and thirty-two miles at a running leap, till he came to the door of the castle, and cried out.

Fin answered from inside, "Is that you, my child?"

"It is," said Fialan.

"Why did you come?"

"I heard your cry, and how could I stay at home, hearing the cry of my father and the Fenians of Erin!"

"Oh, my child, you cannot help us much."

Fialan struck the door powerfully with his sword, but no use. Then, one of the men inside asked Fin to chew his thumb, to know what was keeping them in, and why they were bound.

Fin chewed his thumb, from skin to blood, from blood to bone, from bone to marrow, and discovered that Fear Dubh had built the castle by magic, and that he was coming himself with a great force to cut the head off each one of them. (These men from Alba had always a grudge against the champions of Erin.)

Said Fin to Fialan: "Do you go now, and stand at the ford near the castle, and meet Fear Dubh."

Fialan went and stood in the middle of the ford. He wasn't long there when he saw Fear Dubh coming with a great army.

"Leave the ford, my child," said Fear Dubh, who knew him at once. "I have not come to harm your father. I spent a pleasant year at his castle. I've only come to show him honor."

"I know why you have come," answered Fialan. "You've come to destroy my father and all his men, and I'll not leave this ford while I can hold it."

"Leave the ford; I don't want to harm your father, I want to do him honor. If you don't let us pass my men will kill you," said Fear Dubh.

"I will not let you pass so long as I'm alive before you," said Fialan.

The men faced him; and if they did Fialan kept his place, and a battle commenced, the like of which was never seen before that day. Fialan went through the army as a hawk through a flock of sparrows on a March morning, till he killed every man except Fear Dubh. Fear Dubh told him again to leave the ford, he didn't want to harm his father.

"Oh!" said Fialan, "I know well what you want."

"If you don't leave that place I'll make you leave it!" said Fear Dubh. Then they closed in combat; and such a combat was never seen before between any two warriors. They made springs to rise through the centre of hard gray rocks, cows to cast their calves whether they had them or not. All the horses of the country were racing about and neighing in dread and fear, and all created things were terrified at the sound and clamor of the fight, till the weapons of Fear Dubh went to pieces in the struggle, and Fialan made two halves of his own sword.

Now they closed in wrestling. In the first round Fialan put Fear Dubh to his knees in the hard bottom of the river; the second round he put him to his hips, and the third, to his shoulders.

"Now," said he, "I have you," giving him a stroke of the half of his sword, which cut the head off him.

Then Fialan went to the door of the castle and told his father what he had done.

Fin chewed his thumb again, and knew what other danger was coming. "My son," said he to Fialan, "Fear Dubh has a younger brother more powerful than he was; that brother is coming against us now with greater forces than those which you have destroyed."

As soon as Fialan heard these words he hurried to the ford, and waited till the second army came up. He destroyed this army as he had the other, and closed with the second brother in a fight fiercer and more terrible than the first; but at last he thrust him to his armpits in the hard bottom of the river and cut off his head.

Then he went to the castle, and told his father what he had done. A third time Fin chewed his thumb, and said: "My son, a third army more to be dreaded than the other two is coming now to destroy us, and at the head of it is the youngest brother of Fear Dubh, the most desperate and powerful of the three."

Again Fialan rushed off to the ford; and, though the work was greater than before, he left not a man of the army alive. Then he closed with the youngest brother of Fear Dubh, and if the first and second battles were terrible this was more terrible by far; but at last he planted the youngest brother up to his armpits in the hard bottom of the river, and swept the head off him.

Now, after the heat and struggle of combat Fialan was in such a rage that he lost his mind from fury, not having any one to fight against; and if the whole world had been there before him he would have gone through it and conquered it all.

But having no one to face him he rushed along the river-bank, tearing the flesh from his own body. Never had such madness been seen in any created being before that day.

Diarmuid came now and knocked at the door of the castle, having the dog Bran with him, and asked Fin what had caused him to raise the cry of distress.

"Oh, Diarmuid," said Fin, "we are all fastened in here to

be killed. Fialan has destroyed three armies, and Fear Dubh with his two brothers. He is raging now along the bank of the river; you must not go near him, for he would tear you limb from limb. At this moment he wouldn't spare me, his own father; but after a while he will cease from raging and die down; then you can go. The mother of Fear Dubh is coming, and will soon be at the ford. She is more violent, more venomous, more to be dreaded, a greater warrior than her sons. The chief weapon she has are the nails on her fingers; each nail is seven perches long, of the hardest steel on earth. She is coming in the air at this moment with the speed of a hawk, and she has a kuran (a small vessel), with liquor in it, which has such power that if she puts three drops of it on the mouths of her sons they will rise up as well as ever; and if she brings them to life there is nothing to save us.

"Go the ford; she will be hovering over the corpses of the three armies to know can she find her sons, and as soon as she sees them she will dart down and give them the liquor. You must rise with a mighty bound upon her, dash the kuran out of her hand and spill the liquor.

"If you can kill her save her blood, for nothing in the world can free us from this place and open the door of the castle but the blood of the old hag. I'm in dread you'll not succeed, for she is far more terrible than all her sons together.

Go now; Fialan is dying away, and the old woman is coming; make no delay."

Diarmuid hurried to the ford, stood watching a while; then he saw high in the air something no larger than a hawk. As it came nearer and nearer he saw it was the old woman. She hovered high in the air over the ford. At last she saw her sons, and was swooping down, when Diarmuid rose with a bound into the air and struck the vial a league out of her hand.

The old hag gave a shriek that was heard to the eastern world, and screamed: "Who has dared to interfere with me or my sons?"

"I," answered Diarmuid; "and you'll not go further till I do to you what has been done to your sons."

The fight began; and if there ever was a fight, before or since, it could not be more terrible than this one; but great as was the power of Diarmuid he never could have conquered but for Bran the dog.

The old woman with her nails stripped the skin and flesh from Diarmuid almost to the vitals. But Bran tore the skin and flesh off the old woman's back from her head to her heels.

From the dint of blood-loss and fighting, Diarmuid was growing faint. Despair came on him, and he was on the point of giving way, when a little robin flew near to him, and sitting on a bush, spoke, saying:

"Oh, Diarmuid, take strength; rise and sweep the head off the old hag, or Fin and the Fenians of Erin are no more."

Diarmuid took courage, and with his last strength made one great effort, swept the head off the old hag and caught her blood in a vessel. He rubbed some on his wounds, —they were cured; then he cured Bran.

Straightaway he took the blood to the castle, rubbed drops of it on the door, which opened, and he went in.

All laughed with joy at the rescue. He freed Fin and his men by rubbing blood on the chairs; but when he came to Conal Maol the blood gave out.

All were going away. "Why should you leave me here after you;" cried Conal Maol, "I would rather die at once than stay here for a lingering death. Why don't you, Oscar, and you, Gol MacMorna, come and tear me out of this place; anyhow you'll be able to drag the arms out of me and kill me at once; better than to leave me to die alone."

Oscar and Gol took each a hand, braced their feet against his feet, put forth all their strength and brought him standing; but if they did, he left all the skin and much of the flesh from the back of his head to his heels on the floor behind him. He was covered with blood, and by all accounts was in a terrible condition, bleeding and wounded.

Now there were sheep grazing near the castle. The

Fenians ran out, killed and skinned the largest and best of the flock, and clapped the fresh skin on Conan's back; and such was the healing power in the sheep, and the wound very fresh, that Conan's back healed, and he marched home with the rest of the men, and soon got well; and if he did they sheared off his back wool; enough every year to make a pair of stockings for each one of the Fenians of Erin, and for Fin himself.

And that was a great thing to do and useful, for wool was scarce in Erin in those days. Fin and his men lived pleasantly and joyously for some time; and if they didn't, may we.

The Doctor
and the Fairy Princess
Lady Wilde

Late one night, so the storgoes, a great doctor, who lived near Lough Neagh, was awoke by the sound of a carriage driving up to his door, followed by a loud ring. Hastily throwing on his clothes, the doctor ran down, when he saw a little sprite of a page standing at the carriage door, and a grand gentleman inside.

"Oh, doctor, make haste and come with me," exclaimed the gentleman. "Lose no time, for a great lady has been taken ill, and she will have no one to attend to her but you. So come along with me at once in the carriage."

On this the doctor ran up again to finish his dressing, and to put up all that might be wanted, and was down again in a moment."

"Now, quick," said the gentleman, "you are an excellent good fellow. Sit down here beside me, and do not be alarmed at anything you may see."

So on they drove like mad—and when they came to the ferry, the doctor thought they would wake up the ferryman and take the boat; but, no, they plunged, carriage and horses, and all, and were at the other side in no time without a drop of water touching them.

Now the doctor began to suspect the company he was in; but he held his peace, and they went on up Shane's Hill, till they stopped at a long. low, black house, which they entered, and passed along a narrow dark passage, groping their way, till, all at once, a bright light lit up the walls, and some attendants having opened a door, the doctor found himself in a gorgeous chamber all hung with silk and gold; and on a silken couch lay a beautiful lady, who exclaimed with the most friendly greeting—

"Oh, doctor, I am so glad to see you. How good of you to come."

"Many thanks, my lady," said the doctor, "I am at your ladyship's service."

And he stayed with her till her male child was born; but when he looked round there was no nurse, so he wrapped it in swaddling clothes and laid it by the mother.

"Now," said the lady, "mind what I tell you. They will try

to put a spell on you to keep you here; but take my advice, eat no food and drink no wine, and you will be safe; and mind, also, that you express no surprise at anything you see; and take no more than five golden guineas, though you may be offered fifty or a hundred, as your fee."

"Thank you, madam," said the doctor, "I shall obey you in all things."

With this the gentleman came into the room, grand and noble as a prince, and then he took up the child, looked at it and laid it again on the bed.

Now there was a large fire in the room, and the gentleman took the fire shovel and drew all the burning coal to the front, leaving a great space at the back of the grate; then he took up the child again and laid it in the hollow at the back of the fire and drew all the coal over it till it was covered; but, mindful of the lady's advice, the doctor never said a word. Then the room suddenly changed to another still more beautiful where a grand feast was laid out, of all sorts of meats and fair fruits and bright red wine in cups of sparkling crystal.

"Now, doctor," said the gentleman, "sit down with us and take what best pleases you."

"Sir," said the doctor, "I have made a vow neither to eat nor drink till I reach my home again. So please let me return without further delay."

"Certainly," said the gentleman, "but first let me pay you for your trouble," and he laid down a bag of gold on the table and poured out a quantity of bright pieces.

"I shall only take what is my right and no more," said the doctor, and he drew over five golden guineas, and placed them in his purse. "And now, may I have the carriage to convey me back, for it is growing late?"

On this the gentleman laughed. "You have been learning secrets from my lady," he said. "However, you have behaved right well, and you shall be brought back safely."

So the carriage came, and the doctor took his cane, and was carried back as the first time through the water—horses, carriage, and all—and so on till he reached his home all right just before daybreak. But when he opened his purse to take out the golden guineas, there he saw a splendid diamond ring along with them in the purse with a king's ransom, and when he examined it he found the two letters of his own name carved inside. So he knew it was meant for him, a present from the fairy prince himself.

All this happened a hundred years ago, but the ring still remains in the doctor's family, handed down from father to son, and it is remarked, that whoever wears it as the owner for the time has good luck and honour and wealth all the days of his life.

"And by the light that shines, this story is true," added the narrator of the tale, using the strong form of asseveration by which the Irish-speaking peasants emphasize the truth of their words.

The Thirteenth Son
of the King of Erin
Jeremiah Curtin

There was a king in Erin long ago who had thirteen sons, and as they grew up he taught them good learning and every exercise and art befitting their rank.

One day the king went hunting, and saw a swan swimming in a lake with thirteen little ones. She kept driving away the thirteenth, and would not let it come near the others.

The king wondered greatly at this, and when he came home he summoned his Sean dall Glic (old blind sage), and said: "I saw a great wonder to-day while out hunting,—a swan with thirteen cygnets, and she driving away the thirteenth continually, and keeping the twelve with her. Tell me the cause and reason of this. Why should a mother hate her thirteenth little one, and guard the other twelve?"

"I will tell you," said the old blind sage: "all creatures on earth, whether beast or human, which have thirteen young, should put the thirteenth away, and let it wander for itself in the world and find its fate, so that the will of Heaven may work upon it, and not come down on the others. You have thirteen sons, and you must give the thirteenth to the Diachbha." *

"Then that is the meaning of the swan on the lake—I must give up my thirteenth son to the Diachbha?"

"It is," said the old blind sage; "you must give up one of your thirteen sons."

"But how can I give one of them away when I am so fond of all; and which one shall it be?"

"I'll tell you what to do. When the thirteen come home to-night, shut the door against the last that comes."

Now one of the sons was slow, not so keen nor so sharp as another; but the eldest, who was called Sean Ruadh, was the best, the hero of them all. And it happened that night that he came home last, and when he came his father shut the door against him. The boy raised his hands and said: "Father, what are you going to do with me; what do you wish?"

"It is my duty," said the father, "to give one of my sons to the Diachbha; and as you are the thirteenth, you must go."

Diachbha, "divinity," "fate."

"Well, give me my outfit for the road."

The outfit was brought, Sean Ruadh put it on; then the father gave him a black-haired steed that could overtake the wind before him, and outstrip the wind behind.

Sean Ruadh mounted the steed and hurried away. He went on each day without rest, and slept in the woods at night.

One morning he put on some old clothes which he had in a pack on the saddle, and leaving his horse in the woods, went aside to an opening. He was not long there when a king rode up and stopped before him.

"Who are you, and where are you going?" asked the king.

"Oh!" said Sean Ruadh, "I am astray. I do not know where to go, nor what I am to do."

"If that is how you are, I'll tell you what to do, —come with me."

"Why should I go with you?" asked Sean Ruadh.

"Well, I have a great many cows, and I have no one to go with them, no one to mind them. I am in great trouble also. My daughter will die a terrible death very soon."

"How will she die?" asked Sean Ruadh.

"There is an urfeist,* a great serpent of the sea, a

---

*Urfeist, "great serpent."

monster which must get a king's daughter to devour every seven years. Once in seven years this thing comes up out of the sea for its meat. The turn has now come to my daughter, and we don't know what day will the urfeist appear. The whole castle and all of us are in mourning for my wretched child."

"Perhaps some one will come to save her," said Sean Ruadh.

"Oh! there is a whole army of kings' sons who have come, and they all promise to save her; but I'm in dread none of them will meet the urfeist."

Sean Ruadh agreed with the king to serve for seven years, and went home with him.

Next morning Sean Ruadh drove out the king's cows to pasture.

Now there were three giants not far from the king's place. They lived in three castles in sight of each other, and every night each of these giants shouted just before going to bed. So loud was the shout that each let out of himself that the people heard it in all the country around.

Sean Ruadh drove the cattle up to the giant's land, pushed down the wall, and let them in. The grass was very high, —three times better than any on the king's pastures.

As Sean Ruadh sat watching the cattle, a giant came

running towards him and called out: "I don't know whether to put a pinch of you in my nose, or a bite of you in my mouth!"

"Bad luck to me," said Sean Ruadh, "if I came here but to take the life out of you!"

"How would you like to fight, —on the gray stones, or with sharp swords?" asked the giant.

"I'll fight you," said Sean Ruadh, "on the gray stones, where your great legs will be going down, and mine standing high."

They faced one another then, and began to fight. At the first encounter Sean Ruadh put the giant down to his knees among the hard gray stones, at the second he put him to his waist, and at the third to his shoulders.

"Come, take me out of this," cried the giant, "and I'll give you my castle and all I've got. I'll give you my sword of light that never fails to kill at a blow. I'll give you my black horse that can overtake the wind before, and outstrip the wind behind. These are all up there in my castle."

Sean Ruadh killed the giant and went up to the castle, where the housekeeper said to him: "Oh! it is you that are welcome. You have killed the dirty giant that was here. Come with me now till I show you all the riches and treasures."

She opened the door of the giant's store-room and said: "All these are yours. Here are the keys of the castle."

"Keep them till I come again, and wake me in the

evening," said Sean Ruadh, lying down on the giant's bed.

He slept till evening; then the housekeeper roused him, and he drove the king's cattle home. The cows never gave so much milk as that night. They gave as much as in a whole week before.

Sean Ruadh met the king, and asked: "What news from your daughter?"

"The great serpent did not come to-day," said the king; "but he may come to-morrow."

"Well, to-morrow he may not come till another day," said Sean Ruadh.

Now the king knew nothing of the strength of Sean Ruadh, who was bare-footed, ragged, and shabby.

The second morning Sean Ruadh put the king's cows in the second giant's land. Out came the second giant with the same question and threats as the first, and the cowboy spoke as on the day before.

They fell to fighting; and when the giant was to his shoulders in the hard gray rocks, he said: "I'll give you my sword of light and my brown-haired horse if you'll spare my life."

"Where is your sword of light?" asked Sean Ruadh.

"It is hung up over my bed."

Sean Ruadh ran to the giant's castle, and took the sword, which screamed out when he seized it; but he held it fast, hurried back to the giant, and asked, "How shall I try the edge of this sword?"

"Against a stick," was the reply.

"I see no stick better than your own head," said Sean Ruadh; and with that he swept the head off the giant.

The cowboy now went back to the castle and hung up the sword. "Blessing to you," said the housekeeper; "you have killed the giant! Come, now, and I'll show you his riches and treasures, which are yours forever."

Sean Ruadh found more treasure in this castle than in the first one. When he had seen all, he gave the keys to the housekeeper till he should need them. He slept as on the day before, then drove the cows home in the evening.

The king said: "I have the luck since you came to me. My cows give three times as much milk to-day as they did yesterday."

"Well," said Sean Ruadh, "have you any account of the urfeist?"

"He didn't come to-day," said the king; "but he may come to-morrow."

Sean Ruadh went out with the king's cows on the third day, and drove them to the third giant's land, who came out and fought a more desperate battle than either of the other two; but the cowboy pushed him down among the gray rocks to his shoulders and killed him.

At the castle of the third giant he was received with gladness by the housekeeper, who showed him the treasures and gave him the keys; but he left the keys with her till he should need them. That evening the king's cows had more milk than ever before.

On the fourth day Sean Ruadh went out with the cows, but stopped at the first giant's castle. The housekeeper at his command brought out the dress of the giant, which was all black. He put on the giant's apparel, black as night, and girded on his sword of light. Then he mounted the black-haired steed, which overtook the wind before, and outstripped the wind behind; and rushing on between earth and sky, he never stopped till he came to the beach, where he saw hundreds upon hundreds of king's sons, and champions, who were anxious to save the king's daughter, but were so frightened at the terrible urfeist that they would not go near her.

When he had seen the princess and the trembling champions, Sean Ruadh turned his black steed to the castle. Presently the king saw, riding between earth and sky, a splendid stranger, who stopped before him.

"What is that I see on the shore?" asked the stranger. "Is it a fair, or some great meeting?"

"Haven't you heard," asked the king, "that a monster is coming to destroy my daughter to-day?"

"No, I haven't heard anything," answered the stranger,

who turned away and disappeared.

Soon the black horseman was before the princess, who was sitting alone on a rock near the sea. As she looked at the stranger, she thought he was the finest man on earth, and her heart was cheered.

"Have you no one to save you?" he asked.

"No one."

"Will you let me lay my head on your lap till the urfeist comes? Then rouse me."

He put his head on her lap and fell asleep. While he slept, the princess took three hairs from his head and hid them in her bosom. As soon as she had hidden the hairs, she saw the urfeist coming on the sea, great as an island, and throwing up water to the sky as he moved. She roused the stranger, who sprang up to defend her.

The urfeist came upon the shore, and was advancing on the princess with mouth open and wide as a bridge, when the stranger stood before him and said: "This woman is mine, not yours!"

Then drawing his sword of light, he swept off the monster's head with a blow; but the head rushed back to its place, and grew on again.

In a twinkle the urfeist turned and went back to the sea; but as he went, he said: "I'll be here again tomorrow, and swallow the whole world before me as I come."

"Well," answered the stranger, "maybe another will come to meet you."

Sean Ruadh mounted his black steed, and was gone before the princess could stop him. Sad was her heart when she saw him rush off between the earth and sky more swiftly than any wind.

Sean Ruadh went to the first giant's castle and put away his horse, clothes, and sword. Then he slept on the giant's bed till evening, when the housekeeper woke him, and he drove home the cows. Meeting the king, he asked: "Well, how has your daughter fared to-day?"

"Oh! the urfeist came out of the sea to carry her away; but a wonderful black champion came riding between earth and sky and saved her."

"Who was he?"

"Oh! there is many a man who says he did it. But my daughter isn't saved yet, for the urfeist said he'd come to-morrow."

"Well, never fear; perhaps another champion will come to-morrow."

Next morning Sean Ruadh drove the king's cows to the land of the second giant, where he left them feeding, and then went to the castle, where the housekeeper met him and said: "You are welcome. I'm here before you, and all is well."

"Let the brown horse be brought; let the giant's apparel

and sword be ready for me," said Sean Ruadh.

The apparel was brought, the beautiful blue dress of the second giant, and his sword of light. Sean Ruadh put on the apparel, took the sword, mounted the brown steed, and sped away between earth and air three times more swiftly than the day before.

He rode first to the seashore, saw the king's daughter sitting on the rock alone, and the princes and champions far away, trembling in dread of the urfeist. Then he rode to the king, enquired about the crowd on the seashore, and received the same answer as before. "But is there a man to save her?" asked Sean Ruadh.

"Oh! there are men enough," said the king, "who promise to save her, and say they are brave; but there is no man of them who will stand to his word and face the urfeist when he rises from the sea."

Sean Ruadh was away before the king knew it, and rode to the princess in his suit of blue, bearing his sword of light. "Is there no one to save you?" asked he.

"No one."

"Let me lay my head on your lap, and when the urfeist comes, rouse me."

He put his head on her lap, and while he slept she took out the three hairs, compared them with his hair, and said to herself: "You are the man who was here yesterday."

When the urfeist appeared, coming over the sea, the princess roused the stranger, who sprang up and hurried to the beach.

The monster, moving at a greater speed, and raising more water than on the day before, came with open mouth to land. Again Sean Ruadh stood in his way, and with one blow of the giant's sword made two halves of the urfeist. But the two halves rushed together, and were one as before.

Then the urfeist turned to the sea again, and said as he went: "All the champions on earth won't save her from me to-morrow!"

Sean Ruadh sprang to he steed and back to the castle. He went, leaving the princess in despair at his going. She tore her hair and wept for the loss of the blue champion,—the one man who had dared to save her.

Sean Ruadh put on his old clothes, and drove home the cows as usual. The king said: "A strange champion, all dressed in blue, saved my daughter to-day; but she is grieving her life away because he is gone."

"Well, that is a small matter, since her life is safe," said Sean Ruadh.

There was a feast for the whole world that night at the king's castle, and gladness was on every face that the king's daughter was safe again.

Next day Sean Ruadh drove the cows to the third

giant's pasture, went to the castle, and told the housekeeper to bring the giant's sword and apparel, and have the red steed led to the door. The third giant's dress had as many colours as there are in the sky, and his boots were made of blue glass.

Sean Ruadh, dressed and mounted on his red steed, was the most beautiful man in the world. When ready to start, the housekeeper said to him: "The beast will be so enraged this time that no arms can stop him; he will rise from the sea with three great swords coming out of his mouth, and he could cut to pieces and swallow the whole world if it stood before him in battle. There is only one way to conquer the urfeist, and I will show it to you. Take this brown apple, put it in your bosom, and when he comes rushing from the sea with open mouth, do you throw the apple down his throat, and the great urfeist will melt away and die on the strand."

Sean Ruadh went on the red steed between earth and sky, with thrice the speed of the day before. He saw the maiden sitting on the rock alone, saw the trembling kings' sons in the distance watching to know what would happen, and saw the king hoping for some one to save his daughter; then he went to the princess, and put his head on her lap; when he had fallen asleep, she took the three hairs from her bosom, and looking at them, said: "You are the man who saved me yesterday."

The urfeist was not long in coming. The princess

roused Sean Ruadh, who sprang to his feet and went to the sea. The urfeist came up enormous, terrible to look at, with a mouth big enough to swallow the world, and three sharp swords coming out of it. When he saw Sean Ruadh, he sprang at him with a roar; but Sean Ruadh threw the apple into his mouth, and the beast fell helpless on the strand, flattened out and melted away to a dirty jelly on the shore.

Then Sean Ruadh went towards the princess and said: "That urfeist will never trouble man or woman again."

The princess ran and tried to cling to him; but he was on the red steed, rushing away between earth and sky, before she could stop him. She held, however, so firmly to one of the blue glass boots that Sean Ruadh had to leave it in her hands.

When he drove home the cows that night, the king came out, and Sean Ruadh asked: "What news from the urfeist?"

"Oh!" said the king, "I've had the luck since you came to me. A champion wearing all the colours of the sky, and riding a red steed between earth and air, destroyed the urfeist to-day. My daughter is safe forever; but she is ready to kill herself because she hasn't the man that saved her."

That night there was a feast in the king's castle such as no one had ever seen before. The halls were filled with princes and champions, and each one said: "I am the man that saved the princess!"

The king sent for the old blind sage, and asked, what should he do to find the man who saved his daughter. The old blind sage said,—

"Send out word to all the world that the man whose foot the blue glass boot will fit is the champion who killed the urfeist, and you'll give him your daughter in marriage."

The king sent out word to the world to come to try on the boot. It was too large for some, too small for others. When all had failed, the old sage said,—

"All have tried the boot but the cowboy."

"Oh! he is always out with the cows; what use in his trying," said the king.

"No matter," answered the old blind sage; "let twenty men go and bring down the cowboy."

The king sent up twenty men, who found the cowboy sleeping in the shadow of a stone wall. They began to make a hay rope to bind him; but he woke up, and had twenty ropes ready before they had one. Then he jumped at them, tied the twenty in a bundle, and fastened the bundle to the wall.

They waited and waited at the castle for the twenty men and the cowboy, till at last the king sent twenty men more, with swords, to know what was the delay.

When they came, this twenty began to make a hay rope to tie the cowboy; but he had twenty ropes made before their one, and no matter how they fought, the cowboy tied the twenty in a bundle, and the bundle to the other twenty men.

When neither party came back, the old blind sage said to the king: "Go up now, and throw yourself down before the cowboy, for he has tied the forty men in two bundles, and the bundles to each other."

The king went and threw himself down before the cowboy, who raised him up and said: "What is this for?"

"Come down now and try on the glass boot," said the king.

"How can I go, when I have work to do here?"

"Oh! never mind; you'll come back soon enough to do the work."

The cowboy untied the forty men and went down with the king. When he stood in front of the castle, he saw the princess sitting in her upper chamber, and the glass boot on the window-sill before her.

That moment the boot sprang from the window through the air to him, and went on his foot of itself. The princess was downstairs in a twinkle, and in the arms of Sean Ruadh.

The whole place was crowded with kings' sons and champions, who claimed they had saved the princess.

"What are these men here for?" asked Sean Ruadh.

"Oh! they have been trying to put on the boot," said the king.

With that Sean Ruadh drew his sword of light, swept the heads off every man of them, and threw heads and bodies on the dirt-heap behind the castle.

Then the king sent ships with messengers to all the kings and queens of the world,—to the kings of Spain, France, Greece, and Lochlin, and to Diarmuid, son of the monarch of light,–to come to the wedding of his daughter and Sean Ruadh.

Sean Ruadh, after the wedding, went with his wife to live in the kingdom of the giants, and left his father-in-law on his own land.

Rent Day

Thomas Crofton Croker

Oh, ullagone, ullagone! this is a wide world, but what will we do in it, or where will we go?" muttered Bill Doody, as he sat on a rock by the Lake of Killarney. "What will we do? Tomorrow's rent day, and Tim the Driver swears if we don't pay up our rent, he'll cant every ha'perth we have; and then, sure enough, there's Judy and myself and the poor grawls (children) will be turned out to starve on the high road, for the never a halfpenny of rent have I! Oh hone, that ever I should live to see this day!"

Thus did Bill Doody bemoan his hard fate, pouring his sorrows to the reckless waves of the most beautiful of lakes, which seemed to mock his misery as they rejoiced beneath the cloudless sky of a May morning. The lake, glittering in sunshine, sprinkled with fairy isles of rock and verdure, and bounded by giant hills of ever-varying hues, might, with its magic beauty, charm all sadness but despair; for alas!

> "How ill the scene that offers rest,
> And heart that cannot rest, agree!"

Yet Bill Doody was not so desolate as he supposed; there was one listening to him he little thought of, and help was at hand from a quarter he could not have expected.

"What's the matter with you, my poor man?" said a tall, portly-looking gentleman, at the same time stepping out of a furze-brake. Now Bill was seated on a rock that commanded the view of a large field. Nothing in the field could be concealed from him except this furze-brake, which grew in a hollow near the margin of the lake. He was, therefore, not a little surprised at the gentleman's sudden appearance, and began to question whether the personage before him belonged to this world or not. He, however, soon mustered courage sufficient to tell him how his crops had failed, how some bad member had charmed away his butter, and how Tim the Driver threatened to turn him out of the farm if he didn't pay up every penny of the rent by twelve o'clock next day.

"A sad story, indeed," said the stranger; "but surely, if you represented your case to your landlord's agent, he won't have the heart to turn you out."

"Heart, your honour! Where would an agent get a

heart!" exclaimed Bill. "I see your honour does not know him; besides, he has an eye on the farm this long time for a fosterer of his own; so I expect no mercy, at all, at all, only to be turned out."

"Take this, my poor fellow—take this," said the stranger, pouring a purse full of gold into Bill's old hat, which in his grief he had flung on the ground. "Pay the fellow your rent, but I'll take care it shall do him no good. I remember the time when things went otherwise in this country, when I would have hung up such a fellow in the twinkling of an eye!"

These words were lost upon Bill, who was insensible to everything but the sight of the gold, and before he could unfix his gaze and lift up his head to pour out his hundred thousand blessings, the stranger was gone. The bewildered peasant looked around in search of his benefactor, and at last he thought he saw him riding on a white horse a long way off on the lake.

"O'Donoghue, O'Donoghue!" shouted Bill; "the good, the blessed O'Donoghue!" and he ran capering like a madman to show Judy the gold, and to rejoice her heart with the prospect of wealth and happiness.

The next day Bill proceeded to the agent's—not sneakingly, with his hat in his hand, his eyes fixed on the ground, and his knees bending under him—but bold and upright, like a man conscious of his independence.

"Why don't you take off your hat, fellow. Don't you know you are speaking to a magistrate?" said the agent.

"I know I'm not speaking to the King, sir," said Bill; "and I never takes my hat off but to them I can respect and love. The Eye that sees all knows I've no right either to respect or love an agent!"

"You scoundrel!" retorted the man in office, biting his lips with rage at such an unusual and unexpected opposition, "I'll teach you how to be insolent again—I have the power, remember."

"To the cost of the country, I know you have," said Bill, who still remained with his head as firmly covered as if he was the Lord Kingsale himself.

"But come," said the magistrate; "have you got the money for me?—this is rent day. If there's one penny of it wanting, or the running gale that's due, prepare to turn out before night, for you shall not remain another hour in possession."

"There is your rent," said Bill, with an unmoved expression of tone and countenance; "you'd better count it, and give me a receipt in full for the running gale and all."

The agent gave a look of amazement at the gold; for it was gold—real guineas! and not bits of dirty, ragged small notes, that are fit only to light one's pipe with. However willing the agent may have been to ruin, as he thought, the unfortunate tenant, he took up the gold, and handed the receipt to Bill, who strutted off with it as proud as a cat of her whiskers.

The agent, going to his desk shortly after, was confounded at beholding a heap of ginger-bread cakes instead of the money he had deposited there. He raved and swore, but all to no purpose; the gold had become gingerbread-cakes, just marked like the guineas, with the King's head, and Bill had the receipt in his pocket; so he saw there was no use in saying anything about the affair, as he would only get laughed at for his pains.

From that hour Bill Doody grew rich; all his undertakings prospered; and he often blesses the day that he met with O'Donoghue, the great prince that lives down under the lake of Killarney.

Like the butterfly, the spirit of O'Donoghue closely hovers over the perfume of the hills and flowers it loves; while, as the reflection of a star in the waters of a pure lake, to those who look not above, that glorious spirit is believed to dwell beneath.

The Haughty Princess
Patrick Kennedy

There was once a very worthy
king, whose daughter was the greatest beauty that could be
seen far or near, but she was proud as Lucifer, and no king or
prince would she agree to marry. Her father was tired out at
last, and invited every king and prince, and duke, and earl that
he knew or didn't know to come to his court to give her one
trial more. They all came, and next day after breakfast they
stood in a row in the lawn, and the princess walked along in
the front of them to make her choice. One was fat, and says
she, "I won't have you, Beer-barrel!" One was tall and thin,
and to him she said, "I won't have you, Ramrod!" To a white-
faced man she said, "I won't have you, Pale Death," and to a
red-cheeked man she said, "I won't have you, Cockscomb!"

She stopped a little before the last of all, for he was a fine man in face and form. She wanted to find some defect in him, but he had nothing remarkable but a ring of brown curling hair under his chin. She admired him a little, and then carried it off with "I won't have you, Whiskers!"

So all went away, and the king was so vexed, he said to her, "Now to punish your impedence, I'll give you to the first beggarman or singing sthronshuch that calls;" and as sure as the hearth-money, a fellow all over rags, and hair that came to his shoulders, and a bushy red beard all over his face, came next morning, and began to sing before the parlour window.

When the song was over, the hall-door was opened, the singer asked in, the priest brought, and the princess married to Beardy. She roared and she bawled, but her father didn't mind her. "There," says he to the bridegroom, "is five guineas for you. Take your wife out of my sight, and never let me lay eyes on you or her again."

Off he led her, and dismal enough she was. The only thing that gave her relief was the tones of her husband's voice and his genteel manners. "Whose wood is this?" said she, as they were going through one. "It belongs to the king you called Whiskers yesterday." He gave her the same answer about meadows and corn-fields, and at last a fine city. "Ah, what a fool I was!" said she to herself. "He was a fine man, and I might have him for a husband." At last they were coming up to a poor cabin. "Why are you bringing me here?" says the poor lady. "This was my house," said he, "and now it's yours." She began to cry, but she was tired and hungry, and she went in with him.

Ovoch! there was neither a table laid out, nor a fire burning, and she was obliged to help her husband to light it, and boil their dinner, and clean up the place after: and next day he made her put on a stuff gown and a cotton handkerchief. When she had her house readied up, and no business to keep her employed, he brought home sallies [willows], peeled them, and showed her how to make baskets. But the hard twigs bruised her delicate fingers, and she began to cry. Well, then he asked her to mend their clothes, but the needle drew blood from her fingers, and she cried again. He couldn't bear to see her tears so he bought a creel of earthenware, and sent her to the market to sell them. This was the hardest trial of all, but she looked so handsome and sorrowful, and had such a nice air about her, that all her pans, and jugs, and plates, and dishes were gone before noon, and the only mark of her old pride she showed was a slap she gave a buckeen across the face when he axed her to go in an' take share of a quart.

Well, her husband was so glad, he sent her with another creel the next day; but faith! her luck was after deserting her. A drunken huntsman came up riding, and his beast got in among her ware, and made brishe of every mother's son of 'em. She went home cryin', and her husband wasn't at all pleased. "I see," said he, "you're not fit for business. Come along, I'll get you a kitchen-maid's place in the palace. I know the cook."

So the poor thing was obliged to stifle her pride once more. She kept very busy, and the footman and the butler would be very impudent about looking for a kiss, but she let a screech out of her the first attempt was made, and the cook gave the fellow such a lambasting with the besom that he made no second offer. She went home to her husband every night, and she carried broken victuals wrapped in papers in her side pockets.

A week after she got service there was great bustle in the kitchen. The king was going to be married, but no one knew who the bride was to be. Well, in the evening the cook filled the princess's pockets with cold meat and puddings, and, says she, "Before you go, let us have a look at the great doings in the big parlour." So they came near the door to get a peep, and who should come out but the king himself, as handsome as you please, and no other but King Whiskers himself. "Your handsome helper must pay for her peeping," said he to the cook, "and dance a jig with me." Whether she would or no, he held her hand and brought her into the parlour. The fiddlers struck up, and away went him with her. But they hadn't danced two steps when the meat and the puddens flew out of her pockets. Every one roared out, and she flew to the door, crying piteously. But soon she was caught by the king, and taken into the back parlour. "Don't you know me, my darling?" said he. "I'm both King Whiskers, your husband the ballad-singer, and the drunken huntsman. Your father knew me well enough when he gave you to me, and all was to drive your pride out of you." Well, she didn't know how she was with fright, and shame, and joy. Love was uppermost, anyhow, for she laid her head on her husband's breast and cried like a child. The maids-of-honour soon had her away and dressed her as fine as hands and pins could do it; and there were her mother and father, too; and while the company were wondering what end of the handsome girl and the king, he and his queen, who they didn't know in her fine clothes, and the other king and queen, came in, and such rejoicings and fine doings as there was, none of us will ever see, any way.

The Lazy Beauty
and Her Aunts

Patrick Kennedy

There was once a poor widow woman, who had a daughter that was as handome as the day, and as lazy as a pig, saving your presence. The poor mother was the most industrious person in the townland, and was a particularly good hand at the spinning-wheel. It was the wish of her heart that her daughter should be as handy as herself; but she'd get up late, eat her breakfast before she'd finish her prayers, and then go about dawdling, and anything she handled seemed to be burning her fingers. She drawled her words as if it was a great trouble to her to speak, or as if her tongue was as lazy as her body. Many a heart-scold her poor mother got with her, and still she was only improving like dead fowl in August.

Well, one morning when things were as bad as they

could be, and the poor woman was giving tongue at the rate of a mill-clapper, who should be riding by but the king's son. "Oh dear, oh dear, good woman!" said he, "you must have a very bad child to make you scold so terribly. Sure it can't be this handsome girl that vexed you!" "Oh, please your Majesty, not at all," says the old dissembler. "I was only checking her for working herself too much. Would your Majesty believe it? She spins three pounds of flax in a day, weaves it into linen the next, and makes it all into shirts the day after." "My gracious," says the prince, "she's the very lady that will just fill my mother's eye, and herself the greatest spinner in the kingdom. Will you put on your daughter's bonnet and cloak if you please, ma'am, and set her behind me? Why, my mother will be so delighted with her, that perhaps she'll make her her daughter-in-law in a week, that is, if the young woman herself is agreeable."

Well, between the confusion, and the joy, and the fear of being found out, the woman didn't know what to do; and before they could make up their minds, young handsome Anty was set behind the prince, and away he and his attendants went, and a good heavy purse was left behind with the mother. She pullillued a long time after all was gone, in dread of something happening to the poor girl.

The prince couldn't judge of the girl's breeding or wit from the few answers he pulled out of her. The queen was struck in a heap when she saw a young country girl sitting behind her son, but when she saw her handsome face, and heard all she could do, she didn't think she could make too much of her. The prince took an opportunity of whispering her that if she didn't object to be his wife she must strive to please his mother. Well, the evening went by, and the prince and Anty were getting fonder and fonder of one another, but the thought of the spinning used to send the cold to her heart every moment. When bed-time came, the old queen went along with her to a beautiful bedroom, and when she was bidding her good-night, she pointed to a heap of fine flax, and said, "You may begin as soon as you like to-morrow morning, and I'll expect to see these three pounds in nice thread the morning after." Little did the poor girl sleep that night. She kept crying and lamenting that she didn't mind her mother's advice better. When she was left alone the next morning, she began with a heavy heart; and though she had a nice mahogany wheel and the finest flax you ever saw, the thread was breaking every moment. One while it was as fine as a cobweb, and the next as coarse as a little boy's whipcord. At last she pushed her chair back, let her hands fall in her lap, and burst out a-crying.

A small old woman with surprising big feet appeared before her the same moment and said, "What ails you, you handsome colleen?" "An' haven't I all that flax to spin before to-morrow morning, and I'll never be able to have even five yards of fine thread of it put together." "An' would you think bad to ask poor Colliach Cushmor with the big foot to your wedding with the young prince? If you promise me that, all your three pounds will be made into the finest of thread while you're taking your sleep to-night." "Indeed you must be there and welcome, and I'll honour you all the days of your life." "Very well; stay in your room till tea-time and tell the queen she may come in for her thread as early as she likes to-morrow morning." It was all as she said; and the thread was finer and evener than the gut you see with fly-fishers. "My brave girl you were," says the queen. "I'll get my own mahogany loom brought into you, but you needn't do any more today. Work and rest, work and rest, is my motto. To-morrow you'll weave all this thread, and who knows what may happen?"

The poor girl was more frightened this time than the last, and she was afraid to lose the prince.

She didn't even know how to put the warp in the gears, nor how to use the shuttle, and she was sitting in the greatest grief, when a little woman who was mighty well-shouldered about the hips all at once appeared to her, told her her name was Colliach Cromanmor, and made the same bargain with her as Colliach Cushmor. Great was the queen's pleasure when she found early in the morning a web as fine and white as the finest paper you ever saw. "The darling you were!" says she. "Take your ease with the ladies and gentlemen to-day, and if you have all this made into nice shirts to-morrow you may present one of them to my son, and be married to him out of hand."

Oh, wouldn't you pity poor Anty the next day, she was so near the prince, and maybe would be soon so far from him. But she waited as patiently as she could with scissors, needle, and thread in hand, till a minute after noon. Then she was rejoiced to see the third old woman appear. She had a big red nose, and informed Anty that people called her Shron Mor Rua on that account. She was up to her as good as the others, for a dozen shirts were lying on the table when the queen paid her an early visit.

Now there was nothing talked of but the wedding, and I needn't tell you it was grand. The poor mother was there along with the rest, and at the dinner the old queen could talk of nothing but the lovely shirts, and how happy herself and the bride would be after the honeymoon, spinning, and weaving, and sewing shirts without end. The bridegroom didn't like the discourse, and the bride liked it less, and he was going to say something, when the footman came up to the head of the table, and said to the bride, "Your ladyship's aunt, Colliach Cushmor, bade me ask might she come in." The bride blushed and wished she was seven miles under the floor, but well become the prince—"Tell Mrs. Cushmor," said he, "that any relation of my bride's will be always heartily welcome wherever she and I are." In came the woman with the big foot, and got a seat near the prince. The old queen didn't like it very much, and after a few words she asked rather spitefully, "Dear ma'am, what's the reason your foot is so big?" "Musha, faith, your majesty, I was standing almost all my life at the spinning-wheel, and that's the reason." "I declare to you, my darling," said the prince, "I'll never allow you to spend one hour at the same spinning-wheel." The same footman said again, "Your ladyship's aunt, Colliach Cromanmor, wishes to come in, if the genteels and yourself have no objection." Very displeased was Princess Anty, but the prince sent her welcome, and she took her seat, and drank healths apiece to the company. "May I ask, ma'am," says the old queen, "why you're so wide half-way between the head and the feet?" "That, your majesty, is owing to sitting all my life at the loom." "By my sceptre," says the prince, "my wife shall never sit there an hour." The footman came up again. "Your ladyship's aunt Colliach Shron Mor Rua, is asking leave to come into the banquet." More blushing on the bride's face, but the bridegroom spoke out cordially, "Tell Mrs. Shron Mor Rua she's doing us an honour." In came the old woman, and great respect she got near the top of the table, but the people down low put up their tumblers and glasses to their noses to hide their grins. "Ma'am," says the old queen, "will you tell us please why your nose is so big and red?"

"Troth, your majesty, my head was bent down over the stitching all my life, and all the blood in my body ran into my nose." "My darling," said the prince to Anty, "if ever I see a needle in your hand, I'll run a hundred miles from you."

And in troth, girls and boys, though it's a diverting story, I don't think the moral is good; and if any of you thuckeens go about imitating Anty in her laziness, you'll find it won't thrive with you as it did with her. She was beautiful beyond compare, which none of you are, and she had three powerful fairies to help her, besides. There's no fairies now, and no prince or lord to ride by, and catch you idling or working; and maybe, after all, the prince and herself were not so very happy when the cares of the world or old age came on them.

Glossary

Aoife, Aife (EE fa): the cruel stepmother of the children of Lir who transformed the children into swans.

Aengus Og, Angus, Oenghus: the Tuatha de Danann god of youth and beauty, son of the Dagda and Board (the Boyne River), considered the counterpart of Adonis, Apollo, and Cupid.

Ailell: a popular Old Irish name, the most well known being Ailill, husband of Maeve in *The Cattle Raid of Cooley*.

Beltaine: a Celtic seasonal feast, on May 1, marking the end of the dark half of the year.

Boann, Board: Pre-Christian goddess of the River Boyne. Boann and the Dagda were the parents of Angus Og.

Bodb Dearg (Bove Derg): Bodb the Red, king of the Tuatha de Danann after their defeat by the Milesians. Bodb Dearg is the father of Aobh the mother of Lir's children, and Aoife stepmother of Lir's children.

Boyheen: road, lane.

Cailleach, Colliach: old woman, hag.

Cruachan (KROO ach awn): Seat of the rulers of Connacht; associated with Queen Maeve.

Cuchullainn, Cuchulain (KOO-KULL-in): the greatest hero of Irish myths and principal figure of the Ulster Cycle. He is compared to Hercules and Siegfried.

Currabingo: haunches

Dagda: a most important leader of the Tuatha de Danann; father of the gods.

Dechtire, Deichtine (DECK-tir a):mother of Cuchulain.

Diarmuid (DYEER-mud): leading member of the Fianna; possessor of the love-spot making him irresistible to women; hero of the tale of Diarmuid and Grania.

Dun: fortress, castle.

Fianna: a celebrated band of poet-warriors under the leadership of the mythical Fionn MacCumhail (Finn McCool).

Finn Mac Cumhail; Fion Mac Cumhail; Finn M'Coul; Finn McCool, Fin McCool: hunter-warrior of early Irish tales; central hero of the Fenian Cycle; leader of the Fianna.

Giolla: retainer

Gorsoon: boy

Grania, Grainne: daughter of Cormac mac Airt, the High King of Ireland. She elopes with handsome, youthful Diarmuid Ua Duibne during her wedding feast to the aged Finn Mac Cumhail, thus setting the action of the tale of Diarmuid and Grania.

Grúagach (GROO-agach: long-haired, solitary fairy, sometimes seen as an ogre or giant.

Loch, lough (lock): lake.

Macha (MOCK-a): wife of Crunniuc who brings the debilitating sickness to the men of Ulster, suffered by all men except the young boys and Cuchulain.

Maeve, Medb (Mave): warrior queen of Connacht; wife of Ailell with whom her

Misgaun, miscaun: a lump or dish of butter.

Oisin, Ossian (Uh-SHEEN; u as in but)–son of Finn Mac Cumhail; poet-warrior of the Fianna; central figure of the Ossianic Cycle of Fenian tales.

Ogham: the earliest from of writing in Irish. Letters are adapted to a series of straight lines at the edge of a piece of wood or stone.

Pullilued: worried, fretted.

Samhain (SOW-in): the great pre-Christian seasonal feast, fixed at November 1, the end of the light period of the year, moving into the dark; the one period when the Otherworld became visible to humans. Hallowe'en is the night when spirits and ghosts set out to wreak vengeance on the living. Fires are extinguished and can only be lit by a ceremonial flame lit by the druids.

Sean Ruadh (SHAWN Roo): "John the Red." "shron mor rua" big red nose.

Sidhe (shee): Old Irish; a fairy mound or hill; the dwelling places of the De Danann after their defeat by the Milesians. The ancient gods (the Tuatha de Danann), driven underground below the hill and lake waters, were relegated to fairies in folk memories. In modern Irish, *sidhe* means fairy.

Sidhe Fionnachaid (shee FINN-eh-ee): the dwelling place of Lir, father of the children changed into swans in the story "The Children of Lir."

Slieve Bladhma (Slieve—mountain, hill): Mountain range bordering counties Offaly and Laois, birthplace of Finn MacCumhail, and a featured site in many Fenian stories.

Slieve-nam-ban: mountain in Tipperary, sometimes referred to as Ireland's Parnassus.

Tain (tawn): A cattle raid, as in "The Cattle Raid of Cooley."

Teamair (TOW-er),Tara: " the beautiful hill," capital city of the Gaelic gods; ancient seat of the Irish High Kings.

Thuckeen: young girl.

Tir na n'Og: land of perpetual youth; the Otherworld, home to the Tuatha de Danann after their defeat by the Milesians.

Tuatha de Danann (or Danaan): the people of the goddess Dana. The gods of pre-Christian Ireland who inhabited the land before the Milesians arrived. The Milesians drove them underground. Christian monks demoted them to heroes and heroines, although many of their godlike abilities remained.

Urfeist: greatest beast, monster.